MW00387532

"The process of healing is alchemical ar ~~~~~~~~~~~~~~~~~ are layers to both—physical, metaphysical, and metaphorical. Both the artistic process and any level of healing require creative noticing. Jeannine Wiest's *The Alchemy of Self Healing* will gently help you understand the value of creative noticing to all aspects of life."

—Jane Wagner and Lily Tomlin

"When I began to read Jeannine's book I was struck by her courageous, creative spirit. *The Alchemy of Self Healing* is a powerful read. Each page is filled with wisdom, stories, exercises, and creative ideas to help the reader become aware of their own healing power. This is my kind of book…instructive and empowering."

—Brenda Michaels, host, Conscious Talk Radio, author of *The Gift of Cancer*

"What a cool life Jeannine Wiest has led leading up to the creation of *The Alchemy of Self Healing*. I feel the word "connections" is one of the most important ones in life—and she does as well as evidenced by this lovely and enriching book. If you see life as compartmentalized and yet have an inkling that it is intrinsically all connected—here is a guide to a sensory, juicy relationship with yourself, others, and the world."

—Elaine Clayton, author of *Making Marks*

"Jeannine is the most intuitive healer that I have ever worked with. Her work is body focused but she also channels her vast knowledge into helping you heal your spirit as well. Now through her book, anyone can experience her system! Here is a transformative process that truly self heals. I know that my creative process and my relationships have benefited from working with *The Alchemy of Self Healing* exercises—try the Octopus stretch—it helped me feel lighter—like I physically had more space in my body. Now if you could only get that same space in my closet."

—Tonilyn Hornung, author of *How to Raise a Husband*

"Your body will thank you, at last, a book that gives a creative, deeply insightful way to listen, relate to and heal your body."

—Carol A. Bush, author, *Healing Imagery & Music*, international trainer in the Bonny Method of music centered psychotherapy

"For most people seeking personal growth and transformation, the road to wellness is confusing and the destination unclear. Oftentimes, a road-map and a picture of an end goal is what is most needed to make the struggles worth it. *The Alchemy of Self Healing* is such a road map. By synthesizing diverse mind/body modalities and providing a concrete path of using them, Jeannine Wiest has built a usable and accessible tool for you to begin crafting a new relationship with your body, creativity, awareness, and presence."

—Eric Moya Cst-D, Ms/Mfct, international teacher
and mind/body lecturer

"Cranial Alchemy is the system of tools to cultivate healing and change the concerns most fundamental to us all. Jeannine Wiest helps us return to our inner nature and inner nurture. Make sure you take the time to discover all *The Alchemy of Self Healing* has to offer."

—Alan Questel, Feldenkrais Trainer, creator of
Uncommon Sensing and Pregnant Pauses

"*The Alchemy of Self Healing* guides you to get in touch with your body and your creativity. As a Craniosacral Therapy diplomate I think this makes the book a wonderful resource for people who would like to in-crease the benefits of receiving bodywork such as Craniosacral Therapy. Jeannine draws on her own personal and professional journey, which includes her years as an advanced Craniosacral Therapist, to provide you with tools to create your own personal alchemy."

—Kate Mackinnon, author of *From my Hands and Heart*

"Jeannine Wiest is a genius at accessing the body's innate wisdom for guidance and transformation. In *The Alchemy of Self Healing*, she gives us a step-by-step system for revealing the stories hidden in our cellu-lar structure. So we can make accurate, informed decisions that free us to move into a state of health, wellness, and even enlightenment with awareness and ease."

—Sharon Desjarlais, co-creator of ClientRich.com
and the Manifestation Mystery School

"*The Alchemy of Self Healing* is a true gem filled with transformational opportunities for the reader. I plan to introduce it as suggested reading for my Cellular Yoga™ classes."

—Dr. Diane Sandler, OMD, LAc, CST- D

"*The Alchemy of Self Healing* places itself at the forefront of change. The paradigm shift that is occurring across all healing modalities offers the shift in perspective from effecting change for ourselves in our lives by promises and protocols to the awareness of our relationship to our self, environment and worldview. It is the act of noticing, witnessing and being with our more hidden and unlikeable aspects with an attitude of gentle curiosity, wonder, humor and respect. Jeannine Wiest's week by week practical lessons will facilitate this fundamental change to a natural way of being. I am excited for anyone who undertakes this journey. Welcome Home!"

—Jennifer Absey, RN

THE ALCHEMY OF
SELF HEALING

THE ALCHEMY OF
SELF HEALING

A REVOLUTIONARY 30-DAY PLAN TO CHANGE HOW YOU RELATE TO YOUR BODY AND HEALTH

By Jeannine Wiest

A Division of The Career Press, Inc.
Pompton Plains, NJ

THE ALCHEMY OF SELF HEALING
EDITED BY ROGER SHEETY
TYPESET BY GINA SCHENCK
Cover design by Levan Fisher Design
Author photo on back cover by Starla Fortunato
Printed in the U.S.A.

"The material in *The Alchemy of Self Healing* is in no way intended to replace medical, psychological, or pre-existing care. This material is meant to enhance and support the reader in their journey to wholeness in both health and conscious creating."

To order this title, please call toll-free 1-800-CAREER-1 (NJ and Canada: 201-848-0310) to order using VISA or MasterCard, or for further information on books from Career Press.

CAREER PRESS

New Page BOOKS

The Career Press, Inc.
220 West Parkway, Unit 12
Pompton Plains, NJ 07444
www.careerpress.com
www.newpagebooks.com

Library of Congress Cataloging-in-Publication Data

CIP Data Available Upon Request.

*This book is dedicated to
Mother Earth and all her creatures.
The finned, the furred, and the winged ones,
All, our relations.*

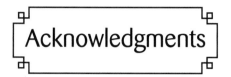

Acknowledgments

Thank you to the ancestors, the D'Aiglons, the Daigles, the Bala-banovas, and to the Khoutieffs. To the Tighes, the Fourniers, all the magical Canadians, the tough yet lyrical Irish, and the dark Russians, I honor you and am grateful for the ancestral soup from which I create and transform.

Deep love for my chosen family, my tribe. Karen Pace, Dr. Diane Sandler, Dr. Rick and Pam Myers, Cheryl Montelle, Evelyn Kuo, Amy Walsh, P.K. Odle, and Lisa Seidman.

Deepest gratitude goes to Lisa Hagan, the best literary agent ever. Thank you for tending to my book as a true book gardener.

Hugs and thanks to Amy Friedman, I couldn't have done it without you.

Air kisses to Sharon Desjarlais for her whispers of encouragement at the start.

To Diana Deene, Ben Kahookele, and Christopher Limber, thank you for your generosity of spirit—I'm lucky to call you my friends.

To everyone at New Page Books, the process has been a pleasure.

To my clients: it is an honor and a joy to create a safe space for you and to witness your self-explorations in healing. Thank you for your trust.

Contents

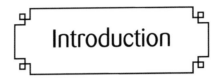

Introduction

Becoming an Inner Alchemist

Symptoms invite us to reconsider our maps, revisit the terrain, revision our journeys, and reconsider our purposes. Finding that the map we have been using is no longer adequate is always disconcerting, even anxiety provoking, but it is the beginning of a process by which we come to a better map, a different terrain, a more considered life.

—James Hollis

Anything I cannot transform into something marvelous, I let go.

—Anais Nin

Alchemy is a process that transforms something ordinary into something extraordinary. Self healing is a birthright, and we all have the option of taking our pain and suffering and transforming it into something extraordinary. *The Alchemy of Self Healing* will guide you to claiming that option.

What are you willing to entertain as possible for your health, well-being, and ability to create?

What kind of connection do you have with your body?

Most people either have rarely thought about a relationship with their body or have developed a relationship that is adversarial. In my work, I encounter many people who pummel their body into shape, ignore it, or drag it around like a badly packed suitcase, often while trash-talking it.

How many times have you heard one friend compliment another only to hear in response, "Oh no, my smile is lopsided," or "Really? I hate my stomach," or "This damn ankle always holds me back."

Every day I hear one guru or another saying, "You become what you think" or "Change your thinking, change your life," and I secretly shudder. Don't get me wrong. My copy of *The Secret* is dog-eared too, and what the gurus say is true.

But there's one caveat, and it's a doozy: If an old story is trapped in your body's tissues or organs, you will struggle to get the results you crave.

The Alchemy of Self Healing guides you toward becoming an Inner Alchemist so you can choose to repurpose those old stories or release them.

In just 30 days you will learn to use the sensory resources around you to release stress and pain so you can more easily flourish in any situation. The exercises and stories offer you a path toward creating a precious relationship with your body, using natural resources that are readily available to you. The rewards you can reap in return for cultivating this relationship are remarkable and juicy, beginning with a deep awareness of connection to the life-affirming natural world.

This book is for you if you'd like to:

- ❀ Respond to challenges with calm, focused energy.
- ❀ Develop habits to navigate the wisdom your body communicates.
- ❀ Transform old stories lodged in your body that drain your well-being.
- ❀ Reconnect with your creative resources.
- ❀ Create your health and relationships "in concert with" rather than "in spite of" existing influences.

The Alchemy of Self Healing is also for you if:

- ❀ You are a visionary, creative, or closet creative person.
- ❀ You are a healer, coach, or therapist who can incorporate this system to augment your clients' results.

Think about it. Who better than you to be an expert on you? All you need is a focus, a decoder, a trusty inner GPS, and a plan.

Do any of the following ring true for you? Are you:

- ❀ Easily triggered by events and challenging situations?
- ❀ On a hamster wheel of stress and feeling overwhelmed?
- ❀ Feeling numb inside; disconnected from your sense of purpose?

❀ Suffering with chronic symptoms that nothing seems to relieve?

❀ Resigned to having no time for yourself or for what you love?

All that can change when you internalize this system.

Each element in *The Alchemy of Self Healing*—exercises, stories, and other tools—is designed to affect the senses, to tease open new health and creative possibilities. Like the process of creating, the process of healing is alchemical. By combining these simple tools, over a 30-day period, you'll become a connected, more creative you. Imagine what your life will be like once you begin to create from flow rather than from stress.

Prior to my work as a Craniosacral Therapist (a detailed body listener), holistic coach, and Reiki master, I was a Broadway dancer, a repurposed vintage clothing designer, and an Emmy-nominated costume designer. Through the years, I also faced many health challenges. In my 30s, coping with chronic pain, I experienced the loss of my internal compass, my inner wisdom.

My own illness and pain led me to Craniosacral Therapy. In time, I healed. Ten years ago, as I began to work with clients to heal their pain—no matter the form in which that pain presented—I also developed my Cranial Alchemy System, the system presented in this book.

There are four parts to the Cranial Alchemy System.

1. Create personal Touchstones—the basis of healing is noticing.

2. Discover your Energy Signature—then identify energy that is not yours so you can work with it, deflect it, or thrive around it.

3. Navigate the Three Levels of Awareness, to help you respond to challenges with calm focus and ease.

4. Track Neutral—a key practice, a game changer to stop you from knee-jerk reactions. Tracking Neutral will guide you to cut through fog to better decision-making, thereby creating a life laced with gratitude and abundance.

The key to living an extraordinary life is learning how to show up for challenges in daily life as an Inner Alchemist. By incorporating the Cranial Alchemy System into your daily routine, you'll give yourself a true, lasting edge for navigating both the wonder and the challenges of your life.

When I owned my clothing design firm, I repurposed intricately patterned vintage linens and silk scarves into art-to-wear dresses and blouses. Though many vintage linens came with embedded stains or jagged rips, when it came to materials and patterns, I viewed them with fresh, inquiring eyes. I often placed vintage cutwork tablecloths on a table to inspect their design pattern. It didn't occur to me to use these linens as tablecloths, although that was their original purpose. Rather, as a sculptor with a block of stone sees himself "releasing" the finished form from the stone block, I saw how the garment could be shaped from the patterned fabric by working around the damage or the stain. Perception creates everything.

I still utilize fresh-eyed noticing today in my work as a healing facilitator. For the past decade, however, instead of silks, linens, and cottons, my material is the body's soft tissues and those connective threads that often are energetic, unseen.

When I became extremely ill and was misdiagnosed with cancer, I came to realize I had to utilize my imaginative self if I was going to heal. I needed to listen to my body, to employ my intuition, just as I always had in my work. Ultimately, Craniosacral Therapy taught me methods for seeing beyond physical symptoms. I realized my body was indeed listening to me.

My ability to go with the grain to highlight a design shape and restore beauty and functionality helps me to assist my clients in repurposing what they might experience as "stained" and "damaged" in their bodies by shifting perspective and focusing on the alchemical possibilities.

My familiarity with looking for alternate solutions also aided me with dissecting a cadaver. During that dissection, and ever since, I saw clearly how everything is connected and that the human body is, in effect, another fabric, and within that fabric there can be found a Direction of Ease.

My mission now, as an expert in combining energy work, Craniosacral Therapy, and creativity, is to open people's eyes to the significance of having a nature-based and metaphorical relationship with one's own body.

I've learned that humor and widening perception under stress, and, yes, trusting that alternatives are available, are skills that can be learned and developed.

Wouldn't you like to know why sometimes you feel great walking into one weekly meeting but when you walk into another, your body and mind leap to high alert? *The Alchemy of Self Healing* not only will help you to understand why this happens, but offers you the tools to make the shift.

High-powered clients who frequently negotiate call this newfound ability their "secret weapon." New moms credit their daily sanity to their alchemy of self healing work. Creative professionals thrive using the metaphorical aspect of this self healing system. And others are able to recover from medical procedures with surprising ease.

The process of learning to cherish your cells is not a race. Whatever your process, honor it. This book is your alchemical guide. I invite you to dive in, to join me on the journey that is *The Alchemy of Self Healing*, and for the next 30 days and beyond, let's find, in what might seem ordinary to you now, the extraordinary.

Week 1

Inner Reconnaissance
and
Creating Touchstones

Chapter 1

Your Inner Reconnaissance

The goal of life is to make your heartbeat match the beat of the universe, to match your nature with Nature.

—Joseph Campbell

Everything is held together with stories. That is all that is holding us together, stories and compassion.

—Barry Lopez

The question to ask yourself is: Whose stories are holding you together? Did you choose those stories or are they your ancestors' stories, an inheritance by default? Are they your childhood shame stories, your "I am less than" stories, your "otherness" stories? If your answer is "I don't know," the truth is this: Part of you does know. There may be resistance to knowing, and in Cranial Alchemy work, we honor resistance. But let me repeat: Part of you knows. And that awareness can lead to relief when you realize that, cellularly at least, you actually do know it all.

The Cranial Alchemy process offers keys to keep you from being triggered and signposts for tracking the changes you yearn for in your life, whether those changes are physical, metaphysical, or metaphorical.

Simply by entertaining the idea that a part of you, in each moment, knows what you need can be a powerful first step. Next time you catch yourself saying "I don't know," I encourage you to add "right now." That's a truer statement.

The Alchemy Quiz: Rate Your Relationship With Your Body

Suffering is optional.
—Buddha

Transforming old, negative stories lodged inside is the key to bridging the disconnection between your body and your mind. Creating that bridge will enable you to create your life, business, and relationships in ways you might only imagine for now.

Ask yourself eight questions to help you track how integrated you are with your body at the moment. Your body is instant messaging you all the time!

1. What part of your body do you love without reservation?
2. How long did it just take you to answer Question One?
3. Which of the following best describes how that loved body part feels? A) Flowing like a waterfall, B) Glistening like sap on a tree, C) Smooth as a rock, D) Sparkling like a crystal, E) Other, please write it in.
4. Now, what body part frustrates you most?
5. How long did that question take to answer compared to Question One?
6. If you could have a conversation with the part you're frustrated with to explain your feelings, what would the conversation sound like? Give a voice to that part and flesh it out (excuse the pun) with as much detail as possible. Does it have an accent? (One unforgettable example: A workshop client's neck had a French cartoon voice.) Does it have a lot to say or very little? Give yourself three to five minutes and see what comes up for you, if anything. Which of the following fit? A) A loud argument B) A tearful monologue C) It's lost in translation D) A gentle whispered, "hello, how's it going in there" conversation E) I can't do this.
7. My daily level of stress is: A) Off-the-charts high B) medium C) low D) stress? What stress?
8. If my spine were an animal, I imagine it would be: A) A quick, gliding fish B) A buzzing bee C) A fossilized turtle D) An octopus E) Other, please describe.

Warning! My tally system is as non-linear as I could create it. The value of this quiz is *not* in the tallied number but truly in your experience of the inquiry. Tally as follows:

- ❀ Question 1: Ten points for being able to identify a body part you love without any "buts." Deduct five points if you chose your heart. There's a chance this is a cop out. Answering "heart" can come from social conditioning, a safe answer that might not allow a more authentic and unique truth to bubble up. You'll know when you re-take the quiz in 30 days. At that point, if "heart" is your true answer, you'll get your five points back.

- ❀ Question 2: If you answered Question One right away, 10 points. Less than a minute, five points. Up to five minutes and you're still not coming up with a part you love, zero points. (All of that will change after you've read this book.)

- ❀ Question 3: If you were able to easily give a description to question three, give yourself 40 points. If this was challenging, great. No points, but we'll work on that.

- ❀ Question 4: Notice whether you jump to an internal part or an external part. Either way, add five points. The practice of noticing can be healing.

- ❀ Question 5: Ten points if it took you a long time to answer this (three to five minutes), zero if you answered right away, and five points if you had to think for a minute.

- ❀ Question 6: Ten points if you didn't draw a blank.

- ❀ Question 7: Pretty much everyone taking this quiz is A or B. Five points for either answer. Eight points for C. If you answered D, you get 10 points for irony. Employing your sense of humor while taking a quiz is both healthy and creative.

- ❀ Question 8: Ten points for any answer and for gifting your spine with imagery. And if you were a fossilized turtle spine, there is a self-help exercise for that in Chapter 6.

80 points or over—The Fluid Alchemist

More than most people, you are in touch with your body, your creativity, and your ability to create. Cranial Alchemy can help you refine the tools you already have and will deepen your connection to the metaphorical, unseen support that surrounds you. You'll enjoy accessing your internal Direction of Ease so you can create your life, health, and relationships in a powerful and juicy way.

40–80 points—The Searcher

You've done some inner work but have either a lack of internal focus or a scattered focus in terms of how you "show up" for yourself and your projects and maybe what you believe is possible in your life. You could use some reliable new tools for whatever transformation you desire. Realizing that you have a treasure trove to search inside yourself is key. Pay close attention to the metaphorical level discussions. Be certain to give extra attention to those exercises that seem most foreign to you.

Under 40—The Inner Apprentice

Work with the exercises in this book and watch yourself grow deep connective roots to the natural world, as well as gain the knowledge to shift perspective and calm your nervous system so you can reach your goals!

Now, put the quiz aside and keep it in a safe place. You may already have surprised yourself with an answer or two, which is good.

We'll re-visit the quiz in 30 days.

Physical, Metaphysical, Metaphorical—What is Cranial Alchemy?

Cranial Alchemy, the sensory and nature-based system I've synthesized, is partially based on Upledger Craniosacral Therapy and my experiential discoveries as a teaching assistant for many Upledger classes. But this book purposefully focuses not on anatomical terminology but on exercises, stories, and tactile connections. Cranial Alchemy's focus is on recalibrating your senses and improving your relationship to your body to the point where you trust your body as a wise ally.

Within this book, you'll be encountering a few technical terms. For example, your reticular alarm system (RAS) is a key element that aids self healing when lowered. Tip: You'll be positively lowering your RAS by doing the exercises in this book and making them habitual. This will likely happen whether or not you understand what the reticular alarm system (also called reticular activating system) is.

Nothing that enters your field of awareness gets past the RAS. As the body's gatekeeper, your RAS is the guy who is holding the velvet rope at a club and deciding who gets in (your body is the club). How you hold experiences determines, through time, your alarm's set point or, in keeping with our club and gatekeeper analogy, your RAS determines maximum capacity for your body: who is on the guest list versus who is attempting to crash.

Is there an abundance of incoming stressors or an overload of trauma to handle in your body? Often we're not aware of an issue until we can no longer compensate around it. *The Alchemy of Self Healing* offers you tools to keep you connected to yourself, to help you learn to listen internally in a nature-based practice so that your alarm doesn't ring off the charts *before* you notice a potential challenge. Instead, the slightest chime of symptomatic feedback from your body will show up on your radar to allow you to offer immediate attention.

As you may already have experienced as you took the quiz, at times internal listening can be daunting. But once you develop a listening, noticing practice, you'll discover internal listening is refreshing. The exercises in this book, offered sequentially, are your doorways to a self-healing, daily practice.

In addition to Upledger Craniosacral Therapy, the influences that have informed the Cranial Alchemy system include concepts I have gleaned from the Four Winds Inka Medicine Wheel as taught by Lynn Berryhill and Tomas Bostrom, as well as creative processes such as those I've adapted from Viola Spolin's theater games,[1] key elements of energy healing work I have studied with animals, sensory musical connections, Reiki practices, and journal explorations.

In the 1970s when I was studying theater games, they seemed artificial. I had no use for them and I had no understanding of their value. All these years later, that has changed, and in true repurposed fashion, with modifications to the original games as they were taught to me, they now shine with authenticity and serve as body-based therapy tools in my work. This is a prime example of discovering a new perspective ("Wow, great tools, that theater mirror game dovetailing with mirror neuron exploration of empathy") from an old story. (Me at 18: "Ugh, why do I have to learn theater games? They're pointless torture.") Even 40 years later, it is possible to reframe anything.

In 30 days you can repurpose old, worn out stories that are not serving you but remain lodged in your body as energy. As you work through each of the chapters in this book, you'll create a custom practice that works for you.

As a healing facilitator, I embrace the idea of being inclusive rather than exclusive, and the work I share with you is a testament to that way of being. Because the holistic premise of my work and this book is that everything is connected, I encourage and seek the connectivity in healing and creative modalities. For me, the exponential value lies in where creative modalities and healing bisect, connect, and converge, sans politics. So as you read, you'll hear about the luminous energy field that surrounds your body concurrently with a favorite qi gong exercise, which just happens to help illustrate that field. Different conduit, same field.

Throughout the book you'll learn to play with three levels of awareness I have culled from indigenous healing practices, and you'll also learn to build from the four tenets of Craniosacral Therapy.

Craniosacral Therapy

The purest definition I've heard of Craniosacral Therapy comes courtesy of Robyn Scherr, an advanced Craniosacral Therapist in Northern California: "Craniosacral Therapy is an educated, specific, non-invasive touch that supports your body's innate ability to heal."[2] The key word here is *non-invasive*.

In this first chapter I offer you right away a few action tools so you can work on your own, utilizing the principles of Craniosacral Therapy. You'll learn what a Craniosacral healing touch consists of, and you'll have an opportunity to begin practicing it.

Why are Craniosacral concepts a cornerstone of exploration with this book? Developing a conscious relationship with your central nervous system is a key to success for the next 30 days and beyond! No other body system has the kind of powerful influence over your well-being as does the central nervous system. But remember, you need not possess an understanding of anatomy to follow this plan.

The Four Tenets

The Four Tenets that underlie everything you do were first espoused by Dr. Andrew Still in the 19th century. These tenets flew in the face of the thought of the time, and a century later, Dr. John Upledger[3] offered a slightly updated version, as follows:

1. The body is a unit.
2. The body is a self-regulating, self-correcting mechanism.
3. Structure and function are inter-related.
4. Movement is health.

The Craniosacral concept of blending and melding with the body's tissues and fluids expands to include working not only physically but also metaphysically and metaphorically. These concepts, along with the three levels described next, are the basis for the internal exploration in Cranial Alchemy.

Undoubtedly there are situations when working with a professional facilitator or health care professional is wise, and in certain cases, crucial. However, all too often we give up our power to experts because, in many cases, we are so disconnected from our bodies, our souls, and gut-knowledge, that it never occurs to us that we have any internal power to affect change for ourselves. As one client recently said, we may feel "blank inside." If that sentiment resonates for you, know that it can change.

The Three Levels of Awareness

"When did you stop singing? When did you stop dancing?" Traditionally, these were the first questions an indigenous healer would ask someone who came for help. The healer would then begin working with levels of awareness. I believe those kinds of questions are crucial, yet we never see them on intake forms.

Depending on the healers' lineage—Native North American or South American—healing work is done on four levels, or with specific connections to nature. In this book, we'll work with three levels of awareness that relate easily to everyday life. What are these three levels and what might they uncover for your creativity as well as your ability to create health and well-being? They are:

The Physical Level—Relating to nature as a matter of daily practice is one component of the Cranial Alchemy system. Within 30 days you may be noticing blades of grass growing between cement cracks as easily as you now assume there's a lack of nature in the city. Feeling depleted? You might not have to wait for a trip to Hawaii for renewal. You might not even have to leave your office.

Helping the body's natural healing mechanisms dissipate the negative effects of stress on the central nervous system is part of the process. Developing the habit of starting a conversation with your organs, with surrounding soft tissues and fluids in the body will help.

If the central nervous system isn't happy, no other system in the body can be happy. By sensorily imaging space within the soft tissue, allowing more balanced fluid flow in the body, you'll allow the body's self-healing mechanism to kick in. Stress-related dysfunctions such as fatigue, headaches, poor digestion, and anxiety can dissipate.

In terms of the body being a self-correcting mechanism—the fewer outside influences such as drugs to mask symptoms, the better. We want to suss out the root cause of an issue rather than mask the symptoms. I am not, however, advocating that you stop taking key medications; rather, I am suggesting that you take these medications mindfully. Chapter 3 covers in greater detail this idea of personal focus.

The Metaphysical Level—According to Merriam-Webster's Dictionary, the term *metaphysical*, which means literally "what comes after physics," was used to refer to the treatise by Aristotle that he himself called "first philosophy." In the history of Western philosophy, metaphysics has been understood in various ways. For the purposes of our work together, we'll refer to the metaphysical level as integration of the physical and the mental, a state that Cranial Alchemy successfully addresses.

Integration practice helps circumvent the fatal flaw of the primitive brain as it relates to the mid-brain and the neocortex. I learned this particular brain model via the Upledger Institute; however, I've also heard other alternative modalities explain it in slightly varying ways. Though some readers may have learned a five-part brain model in school or may wonder why I don't discuss the role of specific brain parts, there are plenty of research books that cover brain anatomy in depth. If words such as "neocortex" make you nervous, hang in there. A valuable brain connection is coming right up.

Cranial Alchemy focuses on the idea of spending more time experiencing and cultivating empathy, bringing that down into our body, tracking and experiencing art and nature at least as often as the time we spend memorizing mathematical tables. To quote one of my former schoolmates, the world-renowned cellist, Yo-Yo Ma: "Because the world economy is so hyper-competitive, much of the focus in education these days from Singapore to Shanghai to American schools is on STEM—science, technology, engineering and math. As important as that is, it is short-sighted. We need to add the empathetic reasoning of the arts to the mix—STEAM."[4] And this brings us, literally, to our senses.

What happens when we ignore our senses and body wisdom, restricting what we feel? Here's one explanation for a whole lot of headaches. Dr. Paul McLean's brain model shows why, for wildly different reasons, two parts of the brain restrict you from feeling your emotions, and instead of embracing what you do feel, you get a wicked headache, or you adopt as truth the notion that feelings are scary and even that they might kill you.

In this brain model (this simple three-part model illustrates one user-friendly perspective but is just one model), the primitive brain controls basic survival mechanisms: eating, gathering, protecting, kill or be killed, procreation, and guarding. You might recognize people you've met who live primarily from a primitive brain perspective.

The mid-brain in McLean's model encompasses all the parts of the brain that have to do with feeling. We will say the limbic system wants you only to feel; feel everything without filter. This level houses the triggers of your family. This area also relates to the mother-child bond, pack behavior, play, and emotional intelligence. The person who works primarily from this area is the person who has no idea she is upset while her upset is obvious to those around her.

The neocortex is the area of the brain that encompasses personality, higher intellect, cognition, and abstraction. People who lead only from this area of the brain are the neck-up types.

The fatal flaw mentioned earlier is this: The primitive brain can't tell the difference between perceived and real threats, so when the mid-brain says, "Feel this," the primitive brain says, "No, I might die if I feel that." And a stand-off ensues. The neocortex is the tie-breaker. It might surprise you to learn that the neocortex sides with the primitive brain. Why? Because the neocortex knows you won't die if you feel a feeling, but the neocortex simply has no use for feelings. So the mid-brain gets metaphorically squished between the neocortex and the primitive brain, resulting in pain.

Although technical explanations are few in this book, I share the McLean model as it speaks to both the concept of old stories lodged inside and those triggers that compel us to act, when acting may not be in our best interest.

The Metaphorical Level—Merriam-Webster's dictionary defines metaphor as "a figure of speech in which a word or phrase denoting one kind of object or action is used in place of another to suggest a likeness or analogy between them. A metaphor is an implied rather than explicit comparison." The metaphorical level is the creative, juicy level. It's where you'll learn to make leaps of connection while remaining grounded and aware of Neutral (a concept discussed in depth in Chapter 6).

On the metaphoric level, we develop our "what ifs?" as they relate to allowing ourselves to strengthen our intuition and imagination muscles. We pull our focus back like a movie camera on a dolly track or a jib crane camera swooping up to capture a sweeping landscape.

In the metaphorical realm, flights of imagination are welcomed. This is the transformative cauldron where changing perspective can become a fun habit, one that is especially useful for confronting serious matters. This level serves to explain why the worlds of *The Hobbit* or *Star Trek* or any number of wildly imaginative books, films, movies, and inventions, enrapture us. If you allow it to, the larger-than-life canvas can stretch your view of your own life.

You can learn to feel comfortable pulling back to widen your focus at the metaphorical level so that you can make authentic connections with archetypes and natural elements. Allow yourself to be fed by that larger and ancient world of mythology, whether it is Greek myth, Indian lore, or the fairytales you heard in childhood. Reclaim that part of yourself or discover it for the first time by becoming familiar with stories larger than your own and utilizing these, when needed, for your healing and creating process.

I was struck by an explanation given on a classic film television channel of a procedure editors call pan and scan; this procedure sizes down wide screen films to fit small screens. The explanation referred to the many elements contained inside just one frame of film. Of course, as an Inner Alchemist, I jumped, metaphorically, to the idea of cells and stories inside us, our internal frames of our life film. The editor described the notion that multiplying the significance of each frame of a scene creates the whole film. Pan and scan effectively cuts off the peripheral side action, which is sometimes critical to the magnificence of a film.

This got me thinking about how we pan and scan our lives. As the editor described the monumental film *Ben Hur*, he spoke about the way pan and scan effectively damped down the extraordinary stunt work with the chariots, so that in the panned and scanned version of the film, only two horses from the original shot are seen pulling Charlton Heston's chariot. In the classic dance sequence in *Seven Brides for Seven Brothers*, pan and scan narrowed the scene so that the joyful, larger-than-life scene grew small. The editor went on to say how the true, full story of these films can only be transmitted on a full screen. Notwithstanding the fact that even small screens these days can be large, the differentiation is valid; even our largest televisions today cannot handle Cinemascope.

Translating this idea to your own life, ask yourself this: What is the peripheral side action in your life that you aren't highlighting, or worse, that you're cutting off because you don't think it's valuable or important? Exploring the mythological can assist you on both sides of your "frame" and function as buoys or wings enhancing what you choose as your life's central action at any point in time. For the next 30 days, image your mythical life in Cinemascope whenever the opportunity arises. Fill out the sides of your life frames.

Archetypes may assist with that filling out. Who do you want at your sides? I suggest you choose an archetype that embodies elements to which you feel connected, a larger-than-life, expanded version to augment one side while filling in the other side with someone you admire, but whose attributes you view as unobtainable. Start with the classics. Perhaps you feel a connection to The Great Mother archetype? She can be the Greek Hera, the Peruvian Pachamama, Mother Earth, Mother Teresa, or even the back of a turtle. Native Americans believed the reason there is a curve to the earth we walk on is because Mother Earth is the back of a turtle—indeed, all Native American explanations relate to nature, and their ceremonies honor visible forces of nature while allowing room for those forces that, while felt, remain unseen.

Or perhaps those archetypes don't resonate for you? Is there a character in *Harry Potter*, the Bible, the Koran, in cartoons that speaks to you? I'm partial to Wonder Woman. I'd just love to wear that belt and have those deflecting cuffs—talk about energetic protection. (And we will in Chapter 3.) Perhaps you're the Prodigal Son? The Hermit? Icarus flying too close to the sun? The Wanderer? Cinderella? Iron Man? Dora the Explorer? The Hulk? Nancy Drew?

I am dropping the possibility of new connective threads just as you might drop a clear pebble into a pond. If you have difficulty with this inquiry, simply recall a favorite childhood story and think about what the qualities are that attracted you to that story. Are those qualities in action anywhere in your life today? Would you like them to be? If you are open to discovery, there is much you can do on your own. That's what the layered exercises in this book are designed to help you with.

For example, the Inner Wisdom can become a lifelong inner compass for you. It's a "tool" you can invite into your awareness during the meditation at the end of this chapter. Once you have it—whether it shows up as an angel, a superhero, scrubbing bubbles, your grandmother, a flower, or a soft shimmering light—you can strengthen your relationship with it and it can become a Touchstone for you. (Touchstones are coming up in Chapter 2.)

One of the Four Tenets of Craniosacral Therapy, the saying "Movement is health," has been around for ages, but for now let's look at it with fresh eyes.

Yoga, Pilates, running, and spinning—all movement, right? Healthy, yes? But let's zoom inside our bodies and meditate for a moment on skin, fascia (the fibrous mesh body stocking that holds physical patterns inside you), then muscles, organs, and bone.

I'm willing to bet you don't jump out of bed in the morning and wonder if your liver and stomach are gliding easily in harmony today. How about whether your cerebrospinal fluid, which lubricates your spine and brain, is bogged down and restricted in its bodily travels. I doubt you've thought about that.

Although movement does encompass the larger exercise moves and gross motor skills we rely on, it is in fact the fluid, *cellular movement*, the tiny yet powerful movement of each cell in our body that keeps us healthy or sets us up for dis-ease.

Take a second to let that thought soak in. There are so many cellular elements that make up even one system of the body; it can be overwhelming to contemplate! So instead of feeling overwhelmed, begin by narrowing your focus.

Simply by placing your awareness or a hand near an area that's in pain—just that focused act—will begin to shift your cells and expand your molecules. And what is a shift? Movement, of course.

Trauma, either unaddressed or toxically held in our tissues, plays a large part in determining if our organs glide easily or are trapped in a freeze-state.

If, as one recent workshop client described, you have a "stuck feeling" in your neck at the base of your skull, know it is not just one element that is not moving. You may feel as if there's just that one stuck spot, but remember, there are layers in your body. Something far from your neck may not be moving and thereby has created "that one pain spot." Some of us know this instinctively, whereas others think if they just press hard on the right spot, the pain will vanish.

There is no magic pill, but every day I see the magic in focused Intention.

By now you may be wondering when your transformational Cranial Alchemy work begins. Perhaps this essay will offer you a workable answer.

Essay: The Flow

Over 10 years ago I spent a week at a goddess workshop on the Big Island of Hawaii. The leaders were strong women with unique offerings designed to help each participant do her inner goddess work. They had handouts and amulets, and we swam with dolphins, and I had a spiritual encounter with a sea turtle in the ocean, mirroring me. But my biggest revelation that week was not on the schedule. It was a dramatic outburst. I revealed my core psychic wound and had a chance to transform it.

From the time we landed at the airport, pretty much everything went wrong. When finally we got going, it was four hours later, dark, and I was squished inside a van with lots of bags and women I didn't know. My plan was to join two friends to find our inner goddess in paradise, but at that moment I felt as if I were the goddess Persephone, tricked and kidnapped by the underworld and on her way to Hades.

I was exhausted after an awful, winding drive, but the moment we arrived at the site, one of the leaders had us draw self-portraits. We were supposed to have arrived for a sunset ceremony but it transformed into a welcome ceremony that included the self-portrait exercise with crayons and colored pens. I chose a brown crayon and drew a bed with a stick figure lying on it. Passive aggressive, but I needed this gooey stuff to stop. I wanted my bed.

After the ceremony, I finally saw my bed. Or should I say, my half of a bed. I was to room with three women, my two friends and the third, a stranger, my new bedmate. I was livid. I stormed down the stairs of this elegant home and fumed, "I am a grown up and I need my own bed." Everyone stared at me, but they did put a mattress out on a private lanai. There I slept without dreaming.

I'm proud that I made sure my needs were met that first night, but I'm not proud of the way I did it. I exclaimed that I was a grown up, but my behavior showed otherwise. The leaders held space for me to rant as I needed to, although the question, and what you'll learn to ask yourself throughout this book is, "Who was running the show just then?"

I know now that my core invisibility wound from childhood was in charge, and the work I needed to do that week was going to happen whether I was a grown up or a child. My outburst, though messy, was perhaps more effective for me than anything the organizers had planned.

In Craniosacral work we talk about peeling the onion. Years have passed since that week-long retreat, and the woman I was to have shared a large bed with is now my best friend. I wonder if I had allowed the evening to unfold in its own perfection, if I might have spared myself the angst of that first evening. Obviously, at that point in my personal journey, I needed the angst, needed to feel something to come up against. I wasn't yet ready to trust the unfolding, the magic of meeting a stranger who would become someone I love. I see the irony now, and I also realize that, however I chose to approach my needs that week, the opportunities to work with my invisibility wound were all around me, starting with the challenges of that first evening.

I tell this story to suggest to you, and to remind myself, that when you arrive at your destination or pick up a book, you needn't wait for the workshop or the work to start. It already has.

The Craniosacral Touch

Throughout this book, you will have opportunities to practice the soothing quality of touch that Craniosacral Therapists utilize. You can learn to use this touch on yourself. If you are unsure about the effectiveness of your touch, you can try it on a friend and ask for feedback. However insecure you may feel, know that, given time, you can develop a sensitivity of touch.

This is the method used in introductory Upledger classes. Start with a nickel. Place it on the back of your right hand. Close your eyes and feel the sensation of it. That is about the pressure you want to apply when, in the later part of the meditation, I ask you to place a hand on specific areas of your body. Try it for a few times. Now switch hands. Do you feel the nickel more on the right or the left hand?

Throughout this book you'll encounter instances where placing a hand on your belly or over your heart will come up. Make a practice of erring on the side of a lighter quality of touch—think of the feel of that nickel or of a leaf floating on water. Play with the quality of your touch.

Here is your first opportunity. (The following meditation may be downloaded at *www.cranialalchemy.com.*)

20-Minute Floor Meditation—Inner Reconnaissance

I've named this meditation Inner Reconnaissance because reconnaissance refers to getting the lay of the land. In this instance, that means discovering your inner terrain. Some people, familiar with getting quiet, are able to dive right in to this exploration. But during one workshop, an unforgettable young participant relayed his experience of frustration as he tried to "see" inside his body. Suddenly he hit upon a solution. Have you ever seen those sportsmen who essentially use their bodies as gliders? They wear special wingsuits and jump off mountains into silent "whooshing." They experience traveling the terrain below in a new way. This workshop participant, for whom stillness was uncomfortable, found a connection to meditation by visualizing himself in a wingsuit on an internal glide, and from that moment on, he was at ease. If you feel challenged by this exercise, try imagining gliding around inside yourself.

As you grow to trust the ways in which your body cues you, you'll come up with your own solutions, your unique way into discovering your inner terrain.

There are three parts to this meditation. Over the next 30 days, I'll be guiding you to refer back to one or two parts during various exercises. This first week, if you feel called to, you have the luxury of sinking into all three parts for the full exploration.

During this first week, I encourage you to repeat this full version at least three times. However, if 20 minutes feels impossibly long to you, by all means try each of the three parts separately.

Part One

Lie down. Make yourself cozy. Allow your body to sink easily into the floor. Today we're going in the Direction of Ease.

When you're comfortable, take three cleansing breaths, which means: Breathe in through your nose and out through your mouth. Make these breaths big, nourishing breaths. Feel free to make sounds when you exhale if you like. Vowel sounds work especially well.

We're going on an Inner Reconnaissance, an inner exploration of your body and how it's connected to nature. Take another easy inhale through your nose and out through your mouth.

Notice how far down inside your body your breath is comfortable going. Is your breath going down to your chest or down to your belly? Just notice. It's your unique terrain.

Now, play with opening your jaw just a bit and breathe in through your nose and out your mouth. Notice any difference? Opening your jaw a bit allows your ribs greater freedom to move laterally and can offer you a connection to belly breaths. If you feel your breath is shallow, just try that a time or two and notice how it feels.

Now let's modify the breathing pattern to inhale through the nose and also exhale through the nose.

So, inhale deeply through your nose, follow the air down the throat into your lungs. Hold a moment. Exhale through your nose. And follow the breath back up and out your nose. Repeat that breath. Inhale deeply. Repeat that process.

Now, image for yourself Mother Earth, however she looks to you. This might be a sphere of the earth or the plot of earth that you garden or the wet sand that you sink your toes in at the beach. I call the earth Pachamama, the Peruvian medicine man name for sweet Mother Earth who will mulch whatever needs mulching in your body. But my choice is not necessarily yours. Why not experiment? Play with imagery. What would you like to give to the center of the earth?

Now, on your next inhale, imagine the energy from the center of the earth is coming up slowly and easily to meet your breath.

Picture your breath flowing in a flexible clear tube of light up and down your spine. And imagine the grounding energy of the earth is following along, rising up to meet your breath and to blend and meld with it.

Inhale easily and exhale. Breathe that earth breath up and allow it to circulate up your spine and around that tube of light. Blend it easily with your own breath. No effort needed on your part, simply see it happening, feel it blending with your own breath. This is a process of allowing.

Now imagine that the energy from the sun, the moon, and the sky is coming down to envelop you and breathe with you. It's come to assist you. Allow that energy to meet your breath on an inhale and blend with your breath. The energy is gliding up and down. Notice how your body allows it or where the energy gets stuck. Whatever your awareness, just notice it.

Now imagine the energy from the center of the earth coming up as well as the sky energy coming down to blend together inside you as you continue to breathe easily.

Follow both the earth breath and sky breath as they swirl easily up and down your spine. When they reach the level of your heart, invite them into your heart. Hold them both in your heart. Just be with the earth and the sky and your heart-breath.

Part Two

Now imagine a circle around your whole body. Turn your attention to just behind your eyes. Start an inner exploration there. Go slowly with your attention through your body, using your senses, asking what you might need to know about the circle that's around you.

What is your circle made of?

What kind of frame do you have around you?

Use all your senses, your felt senses, in this discovery.

Allow your body to show you what you need to see.

What qualities does your circle have? Is it fragile? Is it stretchy? Is it made of flowers, made of colored light? Maybe it's made of stones? A pencil? A stick in the sand tracing around you?

Take your time with this.

Now, softly look down the inside of your body as far as you can see.

Where do you get stuck?

Where do you lose focus or just not connect at all to your insides?

Can you see down past your neck to your chest or is it blocked or maybe dark in there?

Just notice how far you can go, how far you can see what's there. Is it dark and damp? Red and glistening? Maybe it reminds you of a cathedral with soaring caverns of bone and muscle.

Or is your internal body an untended garden? How would you describe it?

Don't worry if this inquiry is hard for you. Just breathe a few cleansing breaths and laugh on your last exhale.

Part Three

Did you know your liver and your stomach move in a cool syncopation? They glide easily, one toward the center of the body and back and up and down in complete harmony when they're healthy. Everything truly is connected.

All the elements of your body are sacred, with gifts for you—creative gold for you to easily mine. Use this opportunity to allow for that possibility as you take your slow moving compassionate focus around your inner terrain.

Check in with your breathing—has it changed, softened, gotten more shallow?

We're doing some detective work—uncovering, wondering, asking.

Where is joy in your body—where does it live? If you feel called to, place a hand on that area and tune in to joy.

How about fear? First place that pops into awareness—it doesn't have to make sense—put a hand there. Offer fear a greeting. Ask it if it has a purpose there in that part of your body. Does it have a gift for you? Something you need to know?

And finally, where is humor? Where does that live inside you? Really use your felt sense—all your senses to feel how it lives inside. Does it have a texture? A color? A sound? Place a hand there.

Take a long last look around, allowing feelings to rise and fall just like your breath.

Thank your body for all the energy and stories it has seen you through and take a few minutes to come fully back into the room, sitting up slowly when you're ready.

Note: In future exercises, when working with Part Three by it-self, you'll add inquiries specific to the exercise or situation or sensory awareness with which you are working or for which you need clarity. This will become clear as we go, week by week.

After this initial week, and once you're familiar with this meditation, you will practice a shorter Inner Reconnaissance each day.

If you're triggered by a feeling, now that you know you won't die from it, you can quiet yourself for a moment and ask, "Where in my body do I feel this? Where inside me has my body been listening and where does it need my attention right now?" *Place a hand softly on that spot.*

Noticing is healing.

Recap of Chapter 1

You took the quiz and have set it aside to review in 30 days.

Concepts

❊ The Four Tenets of Craniosacral Therapy.

❊ The Three Levels of Awareness.

❊ Your RAS.

Tools

Inner Reconnaissance—There are three parts to Inner Reconnaissance. The full meditation is nourishing to experience in its entirety. If you'd like to download a complementary audio of the full meditation, check the Resources section at the back of the book for how to receive your download.

Part One consists of working with the light-filled tube that you imagine surrounding your spine and the accompanying breathwork. However, practically speaking, once you are comfortable with the full process, you may, when time is limited, jump to Part Two, the Circle around You Imagery section or immediately to Part Three, The Inquiry: "Where is (fear, joy, humor) in my body now?" In later exercises, you will be adding to or replacing those words as necessary, depending on your inquiries.

During this 30-day process, I will be referring back to the appropriate parts of Inner Reconnaissance to help you develop facility with working the three parts on an as-needed basis.

Definitions

Felt Sense—This is a primary sense we'll be working with for these 30 days and beyond. It refers to an inner knowing based on sensory data rather than intellectual knowledge.

Chapter 2

Keywords for Your Nervous System

The linear mind loves sequencing. It lives for it. Teach it the sequence of listening rather than contriving.

—Cass Phelps, healer, developer of The Five Signals method

For me the most proficient way to teach the values of collaboration, flexibility, imagination, and innovation—all skill sets needed in today's world—is through the performing arts.

—Yo-Yo Ma, world-renowned cellist

Phenomenology is the study of direct experience. I believe that in order to heal ourselves and foster both creativity and the ability to create, we need to return to direct experience with "what is," in nature and inside our bodily systems. I also believe we can have fun with the process while still allowing our fears to have a say; fear must be permitted its point of view, for if we try to ignore or quash it, it will only loom larger.

Most of us are regularly and deeply invested in keeping the status quo, cellularly and otherwise. Studies have shown that we will choose the familiar at all costs, even if what's familiar is pain. As you experiment with this book and explore your relationship to self and nature on the three levels, as outlined in Chapter 1, you can either anchor your direct experiences or set the stage for transformation. Wouldn't you like to be clear about that which you want to anchor versus that which you want to transform? To do this, you must learn to be clear and specific.

In other words, it's not enough to say: "I want to anchor happiness" or "I want to anchor peace of mind" or "I want to transform pain or creative blocks."

What is unique to you about happiness? Is peace of mind solely a financial condition? Does happiness first and foremost involve your physical safety? Does your joy revolve around the number of awards on your child's bookshelf? Experiment with naming your specific needs and desires from a detailed awareness.

In his book *The Spell of the Sensuous*, David Abram refers to the idea that we've gotten so far away from direct experience with nature—tied as we are to our smart phones and computers—that we ignore that "the body is a creative, shape-shifting entity."[1] Abram goes on to say that "phenomenological research began to suggest that the human mind was thoroughly dependent upon (and thoroughly influenced by) our forgotten relation with the encompassing earth."

Allow that idea to sink in for one moment.

Abram continues: "The fluid realm of direct experience has come to be seen as a secondary, derivative dimension, a mere consequence of events unfolding in the 'realer' world of the quantifiable and measureable 'facts.'"

It is this understanding that brings me to the use of Touchstones as a simple yet intention-infused way to begin creating your new, natural perceptual lens. As you'll learn in this chapter, Touchstones can help you to reconnect with the natural world at a moment's notice.

But first let's bring into this chapter's conversation about self healing an idea derived from Dr. Upledger's Craniosacral work. This involves working with metaphorical stones. We will continue to identify locations of "stuckness" as we did in Inner Reconnaissance in Chapter 1, but now as we build our daily practice, we can add a deeper layer.

Finding a Touchstone

In my office I have the following Dr. John Upledger quotation framed and hanging on my wall: "What we do is take away obstacles, like removing stones from the road."

You are the road. The Craniosacral system, head to tailbone, is the road. And those "stones" Dr. Upledger refers to are often energetic restrictions that are not serving you. Perhaps they had a purpose at a previous time in your life, but they are most likely not helping you at present. I should qualify that statement. Those unseen stones can offer you valuable information as to how your body lost its ease of motion, or how your mindset became anchored the way it has, even how your creativity dried up or got stuck in a rut. In this respect, those "stones" can be helpers, though you'll probably want to transform them or give them a job other than blocking your fluid highway, which on the physical level, is largely your spine.

In contrast to those stones, Touchstones are your friends. They are external, physical reminders of your magical ability to ground, protect, and encourage yourself under varying circumstances. They can be main keywords for your ability to ground at a moment's notice.

Often during an initial assessment with a new client, I'll look at a body as either research in motion or research stuck. Take a few minutes using what you've learned from Inner Reconnaissance and explore the idea of viewing yourself that same way. If that's a tricky idea for you, a Touchstone can help. When you want to feel comfortable relating and listening to your inner self, a Touchstone may prove to be a potent reminder to look at any situation from another level.

A Touchstone can also lower your internal alarm system before you react in a self-defeating way. As an example, when you create a sudden killer headache and, as a result, miss out on a great opportunity, some would say you had self-sabotaged. But if there's an old story trapped as energy in your body, you cannot simply will it away. Your body may well be creating that chronic headache in a misguided attempt to protect you. You'll best work it through by going back to your senses, and a Touchstone may help you do just that.

Clients often express surprise regarding their results in working with Touchstones. "This really works," they'll say as headaches are diminished and tension is caught in developing stages rather than in full blown pain or overwhelming feelings. The process of self healing and the commitment to remaining open to integrate the natural world is not a static state, and at different times in your life, you may find new Touchstones. Touchstones are not to be explained or shared with anyone except your journal. The intent is to keep private the potency of your Touchstone, to grow the sense that your central nervous system and reticular alarm system can rely on it. Discussing your Touchstone or opening its value up to others who might treat it like a curiosity or dismiss it, can dilute your self-healing intent. Trust in the Touchstone's power and make it your own, only your own.

Now, although I stress privacy, in an effort to explain more fully, I'll tell you about my Touchstones. I tend to gravitate toward three. My first is an actual polished stone with striations of grey and gold; it's called a speaking stone. At workshops and when offering my holistic programs, I keep it on the lectern or on my desk. Sometimes I keep it in my pocket. It reminds me of my model of research in motion versus research stuck and allows me at any given time to do a quick reconnaissance as to what messages my body is giving me.

I also perform a short breathing ritual with this stone. This connects me with powerful stone energy that, for me, is alive and resonant. I blow into the stone whatever my concern or dilemma involves. Sometimes I'll use one long breath, sometimes a succession of short, quick breaths. There's no right or wrong way. Because I perceive stones as sacred, this Touchstone works for me. Yours, however, might activate inside you something entirely different, depending on your intention.

Let me give you an example of ways you might employ such a Touchstone. Would you like to calm the butterflies in your stomach prior to a presentation at work? Perhaps you'd like to remind yourself to choose kindness first in a difficult relationship exchange. Maybe you see yourself scoring a goal in a big soccer game? When using your Touchstone, be specific. You're after capturing whatever sensory element is tied to each instance. Try blowing your breath into your Touchstone. Sometimes doing so will feel like a deep "click" of resonance. That's the feeling you want to first discover and then anchor for yourself.

You may discover other ways to connect with stone energy. Touchstones can be lyrical. For example, my second Touchstone came about after an encounter with an Aleutiq tribal artist in Alaska. She showed me how the women in her community utilize story knives. These are made from the leftover bone after the women have hewn the handles for the men's knives—there are slivers left of precious bone and they fashion these slivers into story knives. The women sit with their children in a circle and draw in the earth with the sharp end of the knife; they tell stories of Father Sun and Grandmother Moon. They repeat myths of animals to illuminate their lives. The women weave tales of ancestors' bravery. Their drawings are not elaborate, but connections are made between earth and flesh, and those imprints have a ripple effect on the children. The artist in Anchorage shared her lasting memories of the stories she had illustrated for her children in the earth with that elegant sliver of bone.

I was in Alaska to work on a mini-series, and one day on a 15-minute break, I bought an Aleutiq tribal story knife. Back home in California, I had it made into a necklace. I wear this necklace when I'm writing. It resonates for me and imbues me with comforting bravery. I suppose on the physical level I've imbued the necklace with bravery, but perceiving my story knife necklace as magical is metaphorically nourishing, reminding me of the lineage of Native American storytelling illustrated in the alchemical earth.

I was still working as a costume designer when I was first drawn to this story knife—healing facilitation wasn't yet my calling. Still, today the necklace feeds my life's purpose, a purpose that was, in Alaska, only a seed. When I wear it next to my skin, it speaks to me of integration of seemingly disparate elements, in the way I view Craniosacral Therapy work and the Cranial Alchemy work I've synthesized. The story knife also reminds me that the Direction of Ease is not always obvious, but it is always available. Even the words *story* and *knife* combined in this creative, non-violent way—the simple repurposing of a material used for hunting for the purpose of circle work and illustration—is, to me, divine. And so the necklace as Touchstone for me is a reminder of the alchemy that disparate elements can forge.

The third Touchstone I count on is my Inner Wisdom, an integral element in Craniosacral work. We'll talk in detail about your Inner Wisdom in a moment.

Exercise: Your Fluid Container

Have you ever thought of yourself as a large container of fluid? Probably not, but bear with me here. Being a large fluid container may at first sound unappealing, but the ease of movement of all that fluid is key to your health and creativity!

As not every illness or symptom has a clear cut source, next time an ache or pain appears, why not try finding the "stones in your road"? Or, to modify Dr. Upledger's phrase, why not seek those stones on your fluid road? Alter the phrase to: "What we do is take away obstacles like removing stones from your sea"—meaning your internal sea, your fluid container, your fluid body. The stones are unseen energy cysts, trapped energy that can, through time, change a fluid flow to turbulent waves or to a stagnant pond. How does that resonate?

Here are some ways to look at these watery metaphors:

Imagine the crashing waves inside you creating disruption of important functions. Did you ever think these might show up as such symptoms like migraines, dizziness, TMJ (temporomandibular joint) issues, or even the inability to speak your truth?

The stagnant pond might show up as a muddy and sluggish immune system or as intestinal distress. However the distressed fluid system reacts, whatever distress is created inside, the central nervous system has to make sense of it all. Think about that. What a job!

To start monitoring your fluid container, try the following exercise:

> Lie down in a comfortable spot and do a short, five-minute version of the Inner Reconnaissance you learned in Chapter 1. However, for this exercise your focus is on the felt sense and observation of your fluids.
>
> Become an inner observer to the rise and fall of your breath and the gurgles in your stomach, perhaps the tightness of certain areas

and the places that seem to need attention. Be curious. Imagine all the places fluid flows inside your body, from your skull down to your toes.

If you start to feel antsy or if an emotion scoots by, even if you easily start to sink deep inside your system, say to yourself as you begin to listen closely to your body, "Hmmm, I wonder what's there?"

As you internally do your detective work, don't assume you know how or if the fleeting pain in your left leg relates to the discomfort in your belly. When you find an area where you go blank or feel your breathing change, ask, "Is there a stone in that watery road?"

And once you ask the question, simply let it go. Allow what comes into your awareness without trying to figure out what or why it is.

Most key is to be in curiosity about your internal sea, and if you are, the tide of your health will have no choice but to start to either calm or come to life, whichever is needed.

I learned another way of working with Touchstones, tangible and intangible, during my Inka Medicine Wheel journeys, teaching derived from indigenous Peruvian healers and the work of Alberto Viloldo, PhD. We'll use this modified version during our 30-day Cranial Alchemy work.

Exercise: A Touchstone Walk

In my yard at home I happen to have egg-sized black river stones in abundance. When I give workshops at my home, participants don't have to walk far to find interesting stones. But, let's suppose, before reading this chapter you've never looked for stones. You might prefer shopping for a crystal that resonates with you rather than searching a park or street or forest for your stones. Some of my clients have used the stones from my yard, others have used beach glass, and others utilize stones they found in their driveway or in a mall. It doesn't matter. Rather, the idea is to find a stone that calls to you. Stay on your walk until that stone reveals itself to you. You may never before have imbued a stone (or, in the following example, a stick) with a personal relationship, but you'll see a way to do so.

Say I'm on a Touchstone Walk. I see a curvy, unusually bumpy stick. I pick it up and walk with it. I've connected with the stick on a physical plane. Now I blow my worries, feelings, and thoughts into that stick. In doing so I'm making a metaphysical connection, a melding.

Imagine I take the stick home and wrap it in a silk cloth, maybe give it a poetic name that reminds me of the walk or of my feelings. I place that stick on a display shelf and refer to it often. That elevates the stick to a metaphorical level. It's now become a Touchstone for me, a connection between my state and nature. See what you can find to work with on our three levels.

Intangible Touchstones/Inner Wisdom

An example of an intangible Touchstone, the most uniquely powerful, is the Inner Wisdom we each have but rarely acknowledge. You can, however, connect with your Inner Wisdom on your own. You've already started to by doing the exercises in this book.

Craniosacral Therapists utilize this concept in the somatic work that, from session to session, can and does come up for clients. I've seen this concept adapt well for creative folk, although sometimes not on the treatment table. Interestingly, often when a creative person is blocked, he or she will resist the concept of "play." After working through elements of my system, clients viscerally feel the wellspring in their bodies, a wellspring that can assist the imagination. A client may feel as if she's found her muse that was in fact inside all along. Inner Wisdom help might even arrive via the Inner Reconnaissance exploration discussed in the last chapter.

Throughout your life, the images that come up from your subconscious to embody your Inner Wisdom can and will probably change. They may shift completely or, depending on your challenges, an entirely new image may emerge.

The first step is to get to the point where you allow this information to bubble up from within. The second is to trust that, however it materializes, your Inner Wisdom will be available for you.

This process generally moves in less a straight line than in a spiral. Rest assured, part of you absolutely knows and if you wait for the bubbling up information rather than jumping quickly to linear knowledge, you will be rewarded with glimpses of Inner Wisdom.

For the past 10 years, one of my Inner Wisdom guides has been G., a fantastical bird. She first appeared during a session 15 years ago when I had extreme abdominal pain. My Craniosacral Therapist asked me to ask myself softly if there was a part of myself that knew what the abdominal pain was all about. For a long while I waited. Anxiety and despair hovered near, but suddenly an image of a bird, unlike any real bird I'd ever seen, flew into my mind's eye. Because I'd had practice in my work with Craniosacral Therapy as well as in my years working on film sets, I was able to suspend disbelief, and I allowed the bird image into my session. What unfolded were my feelings of guilt and anger and feeling stupid. When the session ended, the pain was gone. I had a burst of new energy.

Would I have gotten there without the construct of G.? Perhaps. Would mentally understanding the concepts behind it have been enough to rid me of those pains? No.

Those Inner Wisdom embodiments come to people in many shapes, sizes, colors, and forms. For instance, one of my clients experienced Inner Wisdom embodiments as tiny marching soldiers who looked to her like scrubbing bubbles. Another had laser beams of light that danced around her, pointing to areas she needed to bring into focus for herself. Other clients have had angels, grandmothers, a sea turtle, a beloved teacher from the past, and a littler or younger version of themselves. Another had a single, blue-colored light that illuminated his pain and dissolved it via a bath of blue.

Your Inner Wisdom is a "tool" that the Cranial Alchemy exercises help prime you to experience. Trial and error are part of this discovery, and especially while you are learning to trust that it's there for you, know that you may jump to linear thinking. Know, too, that that is the last place you'll find help.

Once you have your Inner Wisdom, whether it shows as an angel, superhero, scrubbing bubbles, your grandmother, a bird, a flower, or a soft shimmering light, you can strengthen your relationship with it through regular, nurturing practice. As you do, it can become an internal Touchstone for you.

My fantastical bird looks like a black, gold, and lilac phoenix combined with crane features. Does that make logical sense? No. *But it makes sense to my body, and my body is informed by her.* That is the crux of what I, on the treatment table (or you, in your living room), need to know.

One of my clients named her Inner Wisdom Joyful Exuberance, and worked with it in the following way. She was doing a nutritional cleanse and was told to take a break from working with me because "energy work" might interfere. I didn't argue, despite the fact that I could not see how Craniosacral Therapy could adversely affect a nutritional cleanse. She was told she needed an occipital base release (a neck release), which she'd had during sessions with me, but the nutritionist suggested she see a chiropractor instead. My wise client asked me if I could just help her on the physical level, and I told her I could set my intention for that, but her body would lead.

During the session, I released restrictions in her neck, and she found the session relaxing. But near the end, she exclaimed "something is gripping" at the base of her skull. "I don't know what it is exactly, but there's fear there," she said. We asked Joyful Exuberance if she had any information for my client that might help us unravel this new awareness.

It turned out that, as an 18-month-old baby, my client had had measles and had to learn to walk all over again. She thought learning would be quicker the second time, and as a baby she was angry and mistrustful of her body because re-learning to walk took the same amount of time it had taken her to learn the first time. That anger and mistrust was still in operation on the left side of the base of her skull. But wait, there's more.

When I asked Joyful Exuberance if there was anything more for today, she showed my client an image of her dancing at age four. My client relayed this image to me. The four-year-old was being told that she was awkward, that she had two left feet. Up until that age my client had enjoyed dancing, but from that moment she stopped forever.

Joyful Exuberance suggested that my client explain measles to her four-year-old self and explain that her unique style of dancing was magical and expressive and nothing to be ashamed of. My client was able to envision the four-year-old hearing this when she asked her what she now needed. As a result, she held the 18-month-old with Joyful and skipped off to have some dancing fun.

My client's pain has not returned since that session.

Now, imagine if my client had just gone for a neck adjustment—she likely would have relieved the pain temporarily, but she would not have found that lasting relief.

Your Body As Vessel

As you progress through this book, try viewing your body as your vessel. In ancient times, alchemists used vessels to contain opposite materials with which they would combine and experiment. They created elixirs and healing potions, as well as attempting to spin the fabled gold from straw.

In body-based healing work, we could say that our materials are old stories, limiting beliefs and, perhaps, spacious feelings mixed into the vessel to create new perceptions. The idea is this: We can mix the desirable while we negotiate with the undesirable. We can metaphorically give the undesirable a new "job" or perhaps release it into the earth. What we cannot accomplish once the undesirable is lodged in our body is merely talk it away. Pretending it's not there doesn't work either.

So, in this alchemical construct, your body can at various times be a cauldron, a cellular soup pot of scraps and leftovers, a hammered silver dish of spices, or a clear beaker of shimmering liquid. The choice is all in your willingness to work with all of yourself, to hold your body as keeper of the answers, the clues, and the ability for transformation.

The following story, "Sparkle Hip," was published in *Massage Today[2]* in 2010 and contains an example of the moment my body "owned" a story. This session also models Neutral dialogue I use as a therapist. "Sparkle Hip" is set in the office of Craniosacral Therapist and Upledger teacher, Karen Axelrod, CST-D. We'll explore the concept of Neutral in Chapter 6.

I use the story of one of my old issues and its resolution as a possible way in for those who are curious about what a Somato Emotional process might look like when working on the cranial table with a professional. It is *not* necessary to cry or relive blow by blow a past trauma in order to move trapped energy! Whether or not you have a specific emotional release connected to the trapped energy, the self-help processes presented in this book will move trapped energy.

This story involved an old recurring core theme of mine. I'm happy to report that it is no longer active.

Sparkle Hip

An ache is getting my attention. I need fresh eyes for the nagging feeling that's been surfacing as a catch-click pain in my right hip. I decide to see Karen, a Craniosacral Therapist I've heard good things about. She works out of her townhouse by the beach.

I find her place easily. I'm early so I drive around and see a Big Lots store. I wonder what leftover retail items I need. I find mugs that say "Official Society of Sarcasm: Like We Care What You Drink." In an existential mood, I buy two, then return to Karen's street.

Two houses up, a gardener starts his blower. A man shuffles by with a poodle that reminds me of my childhood pet.

I enter a small brick courtyard with one cactus, wind chimes, and three sets of shoes. Karen appears wearing an Esalen T-shirt and drawstring trousers. We walk downstairs to her treatment room.

She leaves me to settle in, face up on her table. The blue room has shelves filled with crystals and books. The lights are low. I clear my mind of Big Lots, childhood pets, and expectations.

Karen walks in. I feel the heat of her hands as she connects with the tops of my feet and my cranial rhythm. Her touch feels like sonic electricity humming. She palpates her way up my body, asking me about surgeries as her hands move to my hip bones. I tell her I've had two laparotomies.

"How long ago?" she asks.

"Long ago," I answer. Her hands sandwich my abdomen.

All of a sudden, I'm in 6th grade. A memory floods my awareness as I shift into a Somato Emotional state. I see my 10-year-old self in a New York City bathroom with Heidi. We're both looking in the mirror.

Heidi has blond hair she wears long and straight with a center part, like Joni Mitchell. Her features are angular. She's painting her small mouth with Yardley Pot O' Gloss. A child model, she wears things I've never seen at the Long Island Green Acres Mall.

Today she's wearing a suede two-piece outfit, the exact shade of her hair. The front and back are attached with tortoise-shell rings, so there's a two inch separation on both sides. It's not X-rated because of the brown-ribbed unitard underneath. This picture has been hiding in my right hip.

"Where are you, Jeannine?" Karen asks.

I tell her I am in the bathroom with Heidi. Tears form. My spine shudders from neck to hips.

"What are you aware of?" she asks quietly.

"She's putting makeup on," I say. "I'm pretending I left my makeup at home, but I don't really have any."

A wave of nausea comes over me as I watch little Jeannine feeling less than Heidi. A tear slides down the side of my eye and pools in my ear.

"Tell me more," Karen says neutrally.

"She's a model. She was just in the *New York Times* Magazine section. I ask her how it feels to be in a full-page ad by herself."

My hip screams a raw arthritic pain, but I don't have arthritis.

Now Karen is sandwiching my hip.

"You're asking her a question," she continues.

"I ask questions. I want to imagine what it's like to be in the center of a magazine. I feel so stupid, like she knows things I'll never know."

I fall silent. Karen stays where she is. Tears fill my face.

The observer part of me is pleased and curious about what's transpiring. Being Neutral on the table allows me to be present to witness the trauma unraveling. It's the coolest way to explore.

I'm still in the bathroom with Heidi. I watch her tousle her hair, which is weird because it just falls straight again. It would never occur to me to tousle my hair. "How does it feel to have them choose you?" I venture.

"I don't know," Heidi replies.

Answering me is obviously a pain. I ignore her attitude. After all, she's my friend, and I want to know.

"How come you don't know, Heidi?"

"Because I don't ask stupid questions," she says.

All at once I think, "Did I hear that correctly. What does that mean?"

Then it dawns on me. Oh. Oh no. Grown-up Jeannine, watching from a therapy table 40 years away, sees what 6th-grade Jeannine does in that instant. She leaves her body to protect herself. That day in that bathroom she makes decisions about herself that are stuck in my 50-year-old hip.

Karen notices. "Huge heat release just now," she says. "Feel that?"

"I'm invisible," my 6th-grader cries.

At that moment in that bathroom I confirm something for myself. I am stupid. Heidi wouldn't say it if it wasn't true. I walk into one of the stalls and close the door.

Karen murmurs, but I can't hear her. Louder, she says, "Tell me more about being invisible." Her voice pierces the stall where I'm frozen in 6th-grade fear of discovery.

"My heart," I say.

"Your heart," Karen repeats gently. "What about your heart?"

"She stabbed me with words in my heart."

"Stabbed you."

"Yeah. Heidi, my perfect friend," I sniff.

"What about your heart?"

"My heart is huge and sloppy and not cool."

"Huge and sloppy and not cool," Karen mirrors. "Is that right?"

"Mmmhmm," I whisper. "I have to hide it."

"Hide it. Why is that?" Karen says.

"I have to hide it to make it fit into this body."

I fall silent as a lighter feeling begins to flow into my hip. Minutes pass. My body shifts to take in the awareness.

Through the years, well before that session on Karen's table, I told that story to shrinks and to lovers, pointing in an analytical way to the moment when I decided I must be stupid. None of them gave my body relief from Heidi's words, which were stuck in my hip for 40 years. Now that trapped energy has moved.

Karen asks if I want to reframe the scene. She has one hand on my hip, the other near my heart.

"I'd like to play hooky, take my 6th-grader to the park, and get her out of that bathroom before she has to hide in a stall and pretend she's okay," I say.

"Do you need help with that?" Karen asks.

"No. I'm going to dance out of the building and up to Central Park and 59th."

And then, in my head, I do just that. I feel viscerally how freeing it is to change that story and run to the green trees with my big sloppy heart.

"What are you aware of in your hip now?" Karen asks.

"It feels empty," I say, "like a vast art gallery in the Village waiting to be filled with art."

It's not an analogy I have ever imagined, but that's what bubbles up.

"What would you like to fill it with?" she asks.

"Sparkles," I say. "Lots of sparkly art."

My left brain kicks in. Jeez, what kind of Village gallery has sparkles? Then I laugh, because it's my sparkle art. My hip needs sparkles. The hip has spoken.

I don't know what my Inner Wisdom will show me next, but I'll meet it with a sparkly hip.

Your Body Cliffs Notes

In *The Compassionate Brain*, Gerald Huther, PhD, wrote: "Like all learning capable brains, the human brain is also most deeply and enduringly programmable during the phase when the brain is developing."[3]

For our purposes, we won't examine the groundbreaking research on glial cells being potentially more important than neurons, although I love research that challenges existing perception. Rather, what's important to know is, as Huther writes, "Experiences in early childhood and youth led to the stabilization of certain neuronal pathways. These connective patterns, once they are facilitated and broken in, become easy for our perceptions and experiences to activate— even 40 years after they occurred. They become determinative for 'what goes on inside us,' for how we feel, think and behave in certain situations."

In order to shift this pattern, break down this programming, we might intend to render conscious and acknowledge these already-existing installations. So what does this mean for you? Let's layer this Cliffs Notes exercise and see.

Exercise: Cliffs Notes

Write a bullet point page of your life story through your body, your body Cliffs Notes version. Your body life story is not the sum of the membership cards you have in your wallet or the color of your credit card, or the number of houses you own. Those do not comprise your internal, visceral story.

As an example, my story would start with my birth, which informed my first 30 years; even before I was conscious of my birth story it was recorded in my soft tissues. So my Cliffs Notes might start like this:

- Cord wrapped around neck
- The thought in utero, "I hope the doctors know what they're doing"
- My decision to slip my head left, under the cord, and through

It might continue to my next sensory memory:

- In a rocking chair with my daddy, sun on my face

My next bullet point would jump to a trailer in Lansing, Michigan, dancing with my feet on top of my daddy's feet to "Wake Up Little Susie."

After that, all I truly remember is ballet class—ballet from age 5 until age 10.

So in this instance, in my Cliffs Notes exercise, I easily notice the gaps. I am missing awareness on a sensory level from "Wake Up Little Susie" at age 2 to ballet at age 5. Clearly, during those three years, I was not viscerally "in my body." So this "blank page" might today appear as research stuck in a corresponding area of my physical body.

This is a place to do my detective work, my Inner Reconnaissance. Remember, the body records, it hears everything you experience. The body is not missing those great chunks of time. It's up to you to decide whether reclaiming those missing pieces would be valuable. Then you might either repurpose or release them.

I often see clients who resist tapping into those "missing" body years. In my body-based practice, depending on the situation, in such cases I'll refer a client to another qualified healthcare professional. However, in Cranial Alchemy work we honor that resistance, and oftentimes the honoring eventually allows the client's body to address the needs of the resistance and to work in concert with those needs to release restrictions. The exercises in this book are assembled so that you can work at your own pace and carve your transformed self as slowly or as quickly as your body allows.

What do I do about those missing years in my bodily tissues? Every day I create sensory invitations to my body using my Transformation Circle (Chapter 4), my energy relationship exercises (Chapter 3), and the shorter form of Inner Reconnaissance meditation you just learned.

I begin by asking my body, "What's available to me today? What needs to be seen or heard right now?" Then I wait. I create my daily circle or I place a soft hand on an area of pain. Then I wait some more. I allow. I listen. It doesn't take a lot of time. What time it does take is invaluable as it sets up my day for greater well-being and, yes, productivity.

Depending on what's available to me, how connected I can become in the time I have allotted myself, I inform my day. While my day may inform me—that is, that workshop starts at 9 a.m., I have errands to run, a client needs to schedule a coaching session, there's a dinner party I cannot cancel—no matter how crammed my schedule, I find pockets of time for myself by allowing that I'll be healthier and more in balance if I entertain the concept that *I inform my day* via my body signals. In the long run, that is what's vital.

For example, I have clients with ankle or hip injuries that are healing. For some, the moment they stop wincing in pain, they return immediately to their prior exercise routine, only to re-injure themselves. In contrast, the clients who deepen their body listening skills and ask, "What's available for me today?" ultimately experience longer-lasting results. This is because they are working in concert with their present circumstances rather than in spite of them. That makes all the difference.

I suggest that as you follow the exercises in the book, for the first pass through, follow them in the order given. After that first pass, you might want to mix and match exercises and create your own new habits to support and clear yourself of old stories trapped in your tissues. This is a chance to integrate yourself, to investigate creatively and with ease, to get clues for where trapped energy might be in your body, to free it up so you have more space to create your life deliberately rather than by default, and to trust your gut.

Are you following the Cliffs Notes idea? Why not give it a try now?

Exercise: *My Life Now/My Ideal Life—Color Outside of the Lines*

The Cliffs Notes exercise was a written one. This next exercise is tactile and colorful, thus giving you an opportunity to draw from a different kind of internal resource. For this project you need a large piece of poster board. This is similar to a vision board, but both the intention and the contrast in this exercise lend themselves to grounded exploration.

You're going to divide your poster board into two sections, right and left. Label one section, "My Daily Life" and label the other side, "My Ideal Day."

I have found that some clients doing this project blank out on embellishing their Daily Life side of the board. This can be super important to notice. Do you get up in the morning moaning and move on to drink coffee out of a chipped mug? Haven't thought about it? Well, if that's part of your daily routine—write it on the section labeled My Daily Life. Do you wake up to the gurgling laughter of your baby? Add a photo of your laughing baby. What do you wear consistently, each day? A special piece of jewelry? A backward baseball cap? Custom made boots? A uniform? You may be wearing a uniform of sorts if you routinely dress in khakis and a T-shirt or a button-down shirt. Or do you wear a suit and a silk shirt every day of the work week? As you break down your day and pay attention to where you blank out, thinking, "Well, all I do is work," try putting big question marks where you're unable to fill in the time. Use all your senses.

The other side of your board isn't truly a vision board either because, in this case, the task is to select a specific Ideal Day. After realizing you usually drink your morning beverage from a chipped cup, for example, you may want to find a photo of or describe for yourself an ideal cup—unless, of course, that chipped cup has sentimental value. If you have a laughing baby wake you up and you love that, by all means place it on both sides. When you've been as detailed as possible on both sides of the board, check in with your results.

How many of your elements are on both sides of your chart? What have you had a challenging time with? What was easy and joyful?

I've found that my clients often can detail what they don't want to do anymore, but have trouble with what they do want. They can detail the pain, but can't imagine what could replace pain so they could feel better. Specifically detailing an Ideal Day can be exasperating or it can be fun. Your choice! Remember, Buddha said, "Suffering is optional." No, adding, "I'd go to the beach" isn't enough. Be specific. The beach during what time of year? The Indian Ocean? A black sand beach? Coney Island? Would you swim or sit on a beach chair reading a book? You get the idea. Specifics, specifics, specifics. I encourage you to try this exercise this week and also plan to try it again during the final week of our 30 days so you can contrast your Ideal Days.

People in the film industry have an insider phrase. When something has gone awry with a shot, they call out "back to one," which essentially means "do-over." It's a phrase commonly used when a plane flies overhead or someone flubs his lines or something else doesn't go as planned—just like in life. Just like in creating. This can be a useful phrase for you to remember as you proceed with your healing process. "Back to one" takes you back to where you started. For our purposes, it's a spiral back, not a true repetition, because after each do-over, we have new information, something has widened or softened, we're on a new level of our healing spiral.

For me, "one" metaphysically means, in terms of wholeness now, "belonging in" your body, not fragmenting from it. When viewed in terms of the film business, there is an ironic connotation. One of my film clients actually says, "As long as I don't allow myself to be happy, I'll continue to work." This is a perfect example of fragmentation.

Whether you work in entertainment, or as a doctor, lawyer, or Native American chief, you are constantly creating. The question to ask yourself is: Am I creating by default? If you have a Touchstone and can do your Inner Reconnaissance, you will more easily discover when a do-over is necessary, when you must go "back to one," and what your body and soul need in the moment.

Recap of Chapter 2

Concepts

- ❈ Phenomenology and how it relates to your 30 days and beyond.
- ❈ Ways to discover your Touchstones.
- ❈ Inform your day rather than letting it dictate to you.

Tools

- ❈ Touchstones.
- ❈ Fluid container; start with Inner Reconnaissance.
- ❈ Touchstone Walk.
- ❈ "What's available to me today?"

❀ Cliffs Notes Exercise.

❀ My Life Now/My Ideal Life depictions.

❀ Back to one.

Definition

Energy Cyst—this is a term used by Craniosacral Therapists to describe pockets of trapped energy that, to a trained therapist, have a density to them. As you develop your listening skills, you'll find, as many of my clients do, the awareness of the quality of energy inside your body will begin to become apparent.

Week 2

**Energy Signature
and
Learning From Animals**

Chapter 3

Biography: Your Game...Widening Your Lens

Even when we are supposedly attending to our bodies, we are usually still in our heads.

—Reginald Ray, *Touching Enlightenment*

Awareness changes how we physically move. As we become more fluid and resilient so do the mental, emotional and spiritual movements of our lives.

—Emilie Conrad, *Life on Land*

When I was dancing on Broadway, my friends and I sometimes bemoaned our small roles. One successful actor friend used to entertain us with Shakespearean quips and theater-related stories that I loved. These were usually snarky and funny, such as when he answered the question, "Do you have a match?" with, "I haven't had a match since Charles Laughton died" (in those days smoking was still popular). One of my favorites was his answer to the question, "What did the third spear carrier in *Hamlet* say when asked what *Hamlet* is about?"

"*Hamlet* is the story of the third spear carrier who longs to be recognized by Hamlet and given an amazing quest to accomplish...but he's stuck holding a spear at court."

I love this because it so perfectly illustrates the idea of our lens, of what we choose to focus on, and how we choose to interpret a story.

In this chapter we're focusing on *your* focus. Is yours too narrow like the third spear carrier's and thus missing the larger picture? I laughed when I first heard my friend tell the *Hamlet* quip, remembering the old adage: "There are no small parts, only small players."

Still, we have all had at least one spear carrier moment, a victim moment, a stuck-in-the-pity-party moment. Perhaps we're waiting for a prince to offer us our world purpose, or we're simply watching as life passes us by, or we're assuming that whatever the larger picture, it has nothing to do with our personal situation. I'd advocate seeing the spear carrier position as temporary, but, first, to not miss the point that we are in fact holding a spear (if we are) and perhaps not even the first spear at that!

If spear carrier energy isn't energy you currently connect with, ask your body to show you a way in to a previous spear carrier experience. Use the Inner Reconnaissance meditation, replacing one of the questions there with the following query: "Where is there old spear carrier energy in my body?" Ask yourself where in your body you feel that. Does it feel uncomfortable to even inquire? If so, let's start at that point. Where is "uncomfortable" living in your body? Trust that the first area that pops up for you is it, though remember, it's also fine if you don't tap into the spot right away. As you explore, you'll learn valuable information about how your body responds to inquiry, regardless of whether or not you land on a former spear carrier moment.

Start where you are.

For those readers who have identified one or more moments of spear carrier energy, the next step is to own that you created the reality on the level that your body is speaking to you about it. This can be difficult. You may rail at the idea that you're stuck as third spear carrier and insist that it was not your doing at all. The exercises in this chapter and beyond will give you personal tools to make this an easier and even fun process.

Constructive physical, metaphysical, and metaphorical resolution will follow more easily and quickly if you accept that you did indeed create the experience. Then you can move on to your own quest.

A good place to start is in realizing that *Hamlet*, the play, is in fact about Hamlet, the character. You might ask: Why not indulge the ego if it needs to fantasize that someone else's story is about you? What's the harm? In fact, in doing this there is harm to our spear carrier and his future success and ability to create. In daily life, confusion and disconnection are often caused by relating to an experience only in terms of how it affects us, or relating to it though it's ours to fix.

Here is a key to distinguishing what's ours from what is not ours, energetically.

While perception is everything, if the third spear carrier's perception were grounded with a Touchstone (Chapter 2) and Neutral in his body (Chapter 6), yet flexible and open to a larger awareness, such as the concept of *Hamlet* being about (ahem) Hamlet, congruence would be on his side. If you have created yourself as a spear carrier, this is the kind of spear carrier to be.

As we learn this integrated, Craniosacral, and alchemical way of listening to your body, the energy trapped in the part of us that identifies as a bit player (causing frustration—"I have no lines to say! I have no quest!") is less likely to fester. When we find ourselves in the same kind of limited role to play, we can at least release our stuck-ness enough so that we have the energy to look for a better theatrical agent.

If you have trouble identifying a spear carrier moment, don't worry. This inquiry is dropping a metaphoric pebble into your pond of awareness. I often hear from private clients that awareness or pain relief came fully only after they left the session. The work continues; trust that your body will reveal what you need in its own time.

Here's an example of one of my personal, energetic re-dos. It's actually a re-do within a play about re-dos. In the late 1970s, I was dancing off-Broadway in *Biography: A Game*, by Max Frisch. The play tells the story of a man convinced that if he could only go back in time and re-do a certain party where he met his first wife, he could un-meet her and afterward live a new life. I played a dancer, one of the man's girlfriends to whom he contemplated the possibility of giving a bigger role in his life if only he could leave the party before his first wife arrived.

For me, the most memorable moment of the 12-week run was the night the international ballet superstar, Rudolph Nureyev, was in the audience of the 99-seat Chelsea Westside Theatre. I had to dance across the stage, stop almost directly in front of where he was sitting, and execute a deep plié. I wasn't bad, but as I rose from the plié, my torso leaned forward just enough to break an otherwise perfect, balletic line. I heard a snort. I jeté-d quickly offstage right, my heart pounding.

My personal re-do involved remaining calm and saying with a laugh, "Oh yes, the night I danced for Nureyev…"

That moment, thankfully, is not lodged inside me as stuck energy. I can easily think about it, and when I do, for a moment, I am right back in that upstairs theatre on 43rd Street, down to the resin smell of its floors. No change in blood pressure, no internal protective alarm starts, and no trigger. That moment, thankfully, remains just a story.

Clients often ask me what makes one memory deeply affect our body and another become simply a good story? The answer is unique for each person, because each unique life has its corresponding triggers and held beliefs. Still, the importance of knowing and understanding the difference between energy inside and outside oneself is universal.

When you can identify the quality of energy in charge inside you, you can determine the level of connection on which you want to engage. You have choices. When you are blindly triggered by a situation, you no longer have any choice.

That night in front of Nureyev, I knew I wasn't trying to be a prima ballerina. The energy in my body was storytelling energy. Bummer about the plié, but the snort was all Nureyev's energy, his relating to what he knew how to do at that stage of his life—criticize dancers. My energy in the moment was benign—I was only playing a ballerina, not trying to be one, and any energy trapped was swiftly dissipated when I laughed about the snort. I felt no shame. Instinctively I knew Nureyev's snort of disgust at my form had nothing to do with my identity. It was he, not me, who was invested in ballet, and indeed, after the show, at Studio 54 with friends and colleagues, I had fun sharing the story.

Now, you might be thinking about the "Sparkle Hip" essay in the last chapter. It would be logical for you to ask how a girl in 6th grade hurt me so much more deeply than had an international ballet superstar, but by now I hope you see that logic has nothing to do with whether or not energy gets stuck inside us.

This is why it is vital for us to allow whatever comes up in this work—even if it seems too small to pay attention to, even if it strikes you as being far from what you think you need to work on, even if it seems to you barely worth jotting down in a journal. Your life experiences are all grist for the mill. Just make sure you are the one doing the milling! Or the re-milling.

Our biographies are truly ours to play with, and it is our responsibility to take care with how we do this. If, for instance, you tell yourself an old story that revolves around the notion that no matter what you do, "that's just the way it is," and the ending will always be the same, the universe will eventually show you exactly that.

Or if life in the present moment shows you a different possible ending, you'll fail to see it or you'll see that different ending and it will arouse only discomfort.

As long as you unknowingly follow the script currently written in your soft tissues, you'll continue to create a limited, confined life story. Those limits, that confinement, starts with trauma, limited beliefs absorbed early on in life, or thoughts, but ultimately hits the body with the words we choose to use to describe the experience. For instance, think of these lines, culled from clients, and what they are telling the body:

- ❀ "I'm not built for this."
- ❀ "That's the way life is."
- ❀ "It hasn't killed me yet."

Here's what your body hears (for each of the previous lines):

- ❀ "I can't ever physically do this."
- ❀ "Life is pre-determined, so why bother."
- ❀ "I will die from this."

One way of turning those lines around is to deliberately craft an opposite statement. This may remind you of doing affirmations, but sometimes affirmations can have a "fake-it-'til-you-make-it" quality about them, or they can be sweeping generalities and a danger exists that you'll connect only from the neck up. We don't want to miss out on crucial body-based information. In this work, the re-working of words is only a start, a jumping-off point for inner soft tissue, fluid exploration, and deep listening.

When it comes to listening to your body, you can't fake anything, not even the smallest lie gets by for long. You can't merely override destructive words imprinted in your cellular body by using abundant words and expect huge changes in your life. I'm all for using words of abundance and gratitude, but in my practice, I've noticed that affirmations alone seldom reliably offer the desired results. Used as a jumping-off point, however, they're powerful.

How do you reframe a line like, "Well, it hasn't killed me?" You might say instead, "Is this worth dying for?" Of course that's just one reframe; however, by changing the statement into a question, you've opened yourself up to possibilities.

Beyond that one simple change, you've also received the opportunity to take the question to your body via Inner Reconnaissance and your Touchstones and to ask for sensory feedback and clarity around this further question:

"Is there *a purpose* for this belief or this trapped energy, a job that it thinks it needs to do in my body?"

In the example of "It hasn't killed me yet," there might be a badge of courage or honor attached ("I can withstand anything") that could qualify as a "job." Let's say the "it" in the phrase was neck pain—neck pain hasn't killed me yet. You now have a specific place to inquire, and so you might place your hand lightly on your neck, relax, and wait, staying open to notice any changes there.

These changes can show up as temperature changes, breath changes, stomach rumbling, a softening or a sense of lengthening of muscles or other body tissues. Should these occur, you'll know your body, the affected area and more, has felt heard. That is an example of the difference between affirmations and this work. In the first case, you make only a verbal declaration of a wished outcome, whereas here you have a ripple effect throughout your body to track plus a potential re-boot of the body's self-healing mechanism. Of course, just recognizing the damage those words set you up for might be all the wake-up call you need. Still, if that thread, that phrase, is deeply ingrained, you have Cranial Alchemy work to do.

Here are some other questions you can ask your body during your inquiry process, questions that can offer up body-based information:

- ❀ When do you remember first hearing the phrase?
- ❀ How old were you?
- ❀ Where were you?
- ❀ Who said those words to you?

Again, trust what pops up for you first. Integrating the exercises and concepts in this book can go a long way to releasing old attachments trapped in your body.

It is possible, of course, to start a transformation process of certain limiting ideas by reframing the way we speak of them. Whether or not you can do that successfully will depend on your specificity, your attention to detail, and authentic-to-you word selection. Your intention is paramount. Be deliberate. Notice that words can convey similar messages on one level but not on another. As an example, an Upledger mentor of mine suggested that instead of saying, "Don't spill your milk," you might try, "Be careful with your milk."

I invite you to re-read those two statements. In between, take a breath and pause. Can you feel into—listen on a sensory level—the difference in those two statements? There is a tightness, a clipped sharpness to the first statement that presupposes something bad will happen soon and it will be all your fault. Can you resonate with how much less milk might be spilled worldwide if children heard, "Be careful with" instead of, "Don't spill"? There is a key distinction between the two phrases and also a large ripple effect in terms of how each statement is absorbed by the body. The body/mind cannot process a negative statement like, "Don't spill your milk." It can, however, absorb "Be careful..."—a positive, action statement.

Many of my clients have, as their underlying childhood mantra, some version of "I was never good enough for my parents (or teachers)." Never smart enough, pretty enough, or tough enough. The list of how we each own "faults" that are rarely ours, distances us from our gut knowing.

Conversely, I have clients who grew up excelling at everything: the brightest, fastest, and most talented. When faced with a pain message from the body that all is not well, they panic. "This can't happen, not to me," they'll say as they determine that they must achieve their prior state of perceived perfection. Railing at physical reality only compounds the existing pain. The process of healing is not, in itself, a race, and yet I see many clients whose expectations of how their body should heal cloud the advances their body is prepared to make.

No wonder many of us grow up with fractured relationships with our body. Joshua Boettiger wrote in *Parabola Magazine* that "we suffer under the language of verticality" referring to our "God-language."[1] The idea in many religions is that descending is "going into the body," which historically has been seen as a negative. However, as the notion relates to healing body/mind fragmentation, I'd say that descent into the body is just what's in order, whether or not you're religious.

The Jewish Torah's story of Isaac's digging of the wells[2] supplies good imagery to use with Cranial Alchemy exploration. The story illustrates that even if the wells you dig become covered up, with perseverance, with time, we can dig fresh wells and we will break through to water. As Boettiger writes, "Water represents nourishment, sustenance, source. While each of us has our own specific place to dig, the water we access is the universal."[3]

Try working with your physical internal body as a wellspring in the exercises. To locate "the right spot" we might even imagine cerebrospinal fluid as the universal fluid we all access. Remember, in the well analogy, you are the bucket—the conduit, accessing source as it reveals itself to you.

The Luminous Energy Field

In the Western religious, historically linear view of the body, up toward heaven is good; down into the body is bad. In contrast, indigenous medicine men, and many energy-based alternative healers and facilitators work with an elongated donut shape, known as a torus shape, around the body. It's the unseen but real luminous energy field that surrounds each of us. Let's include the concept of the luminous energy field in our quest to befriend our body. Think of the halo surrounding a saint's head, or the large feathered Native Americans' aura-like headdresses worn only by elder wise ones. Some relate this to the energy that emanates from chakra fields, and some experience this field as an energetic type of protection, whereas others view it simply as a way of embracing the unseen aspects of themselves. In every culture, the idea exists in some form.

Your first introduction to this idea came during the second half of the Inner Reconnaissance meditation when you were asked to see a circle around your body. Now, allow this new layer of information to inform your next Inner Reconnaissance practice. See how your experience unfolds. This field has no sharp corners, no disconnection from source. Medicine men work within this field, which can retain the old stories, ancestral debris, and imprints of the past that are not serving you. You can work with them as well, as you season your sensory perceptions.

Exercise One—Bringing Down Heaven

This is a qi gong exercise that is a favorite in my workshops.

Stand with feet shoulder-width apart. Check to make sure your knees are soft, not locked. Slowly bring your arms out to the side, imagining a bellows expanding or that you're making a snow angel (Figure 3-1). The key is to only move as fast as you can while staying aware of *the space you are*

Figure 3-1

Figure 3-2

Figure 3-3

moving through, not your arms moving. This is not calisthenics! (Hint: you'll be moving slowly.)

Now, as your arms reach shoulder height, turn your palms upward toward the sky and continue moving your arms upward (Figure 3-2) until they meet above your head in an egg shape. Next, keeping that shape, turn your palms so they face your face. Bring your arms down very slowly, fingertips touching each other. The focus is wide here.

The trick is that as you move your arms down, I want you to be aware not only of the space in front of you, but to imagine a pair of arms coming down behind you, mirroring the action in the front (Figure 3-3). The idea is to bring recognition to the back of your body. That's a whole area of your energy field that is often overlooked. Any lack of inclusion of this part of your posterior field represents energetic currency that belongs to you, yet is wasted.

Repeat *Bringing Down Heaven* a total of three times.

Once you get the hang of it, Bringing Down Heaven is a great way to wake yourself up to what unseen resources belong to you, both literally and figuratively. With a different intention, it's also a great grounding exercise that can be completed in less than five minutes.

Bringing Down Heaven can smooth your luminous field. Try the exercise with that intent for one round and notice what comes into your awareness, if there are any differences with a different intention.

Years ago, I worked with a client who exhibited an extreme example of what happens when we refuse to see what effect our words have on our bodies, when we refuse to land inside our body and dig our well. This man had millions of dollars, a wonderful family, multiple houses, and the freedom to travel wherever he wished, but he trusted no one. Unfortunately, that mistrust extended to his own body that began to fail him. He was terrified of becoming a cripple who would not be able to continue to enjoy the fabulous over-the-top lifestyle he had customarily enjoyed.

When I first began to work with him, doing a hands-on cranial assessment, I was impressed by the sensory image of his spine "running away from home." Of course, this wasn't a technical assessment, but the spine is the back of the mind, metaphorically speaking, and I sensed that his spine had become disfigured as a means of moving/twisting away from feeling or dealing with his life.

His spine had curved so far away "from home" that one hip had actually become part of his waist measurement in a tuxedo fitting. He thought he simply must be gaining weight, and though I said nothing, I realized this was an extreme example of someone refusing to listen to his body.

As we worked together, I discovered that everyone around him told him precisely what he wanted to hear.

The only signals warning him against certain ideas and behaviors were coming from his own body, but he was trying to run it as though it were separate from himself, something "other" that must submit to his will the way other people did—as though his body were an employee he needed to replace. I understood that his paradigm would have to shift in order for his pain to transform. Sadly, he died without ever having attained that understanding.

That was an extreme example, but through the years, many clients have come to me with a disassociation from their bodies. From a body's point of view, there's a perceived good reason to disassociate. In fact, often the body thinks it's protecting or helping whereas it's merely following an old story as though that story is still happening. In a way, on one of the three levels, that story is still running. As a body listener, I facilitate the process of discovering on the treatment table what that cellular reason is for that story being stuck. But you can do your own Inner Reconnaissance (Chapter 1) and now add the layers in this chapter to deepen that initial go-round. It's a matter of beginning to listen even more closely, of listening internally, and once you have the hang of that, of experimenting with clear intention.

Questions arise, of course. For instance, how do you know what's yours and what is "other"? Equally important is finding ways to discover when you are running your life and when your life is running you. One of the best ways to do this is to practice the following energy exercises. With these exercises, we're moving further into the realm of the intangible, a place for you to learn a new, metaphorical awareness level. It's important that you be patient with yourself through this learning process.

Energy Signature

Your Energy Signature is critical to know so you can shift and heal. This is key in order for you to make decisions that are truly in line with your deepest knowing, your Inner Wisdom. The exercises in this chapter will have you relating to others, to nature, to the unfamiliar, to place, and to the world. Each of these exercises will act as a doorway to discovering and identifying your Energy Signature. Though I will outline general categories of sample client Energy Signatures, yours will be as unique as your fingerprint. Here are a few types:

1. Kinetic, in motion, quick and sharp, verbally cuts to the chase.
2. Deliberate, slow careful movements, weighs all possibilities before engaging verbally.

3. Easy, breezy, floats into the room, a light but magnetic force, everything effortless; you don't remember what they say, just how much at ease they make you feel.

Sometimes your Energy Signature is clear to everyone but you. For example, for years before I was a holistic facilitator, I often heard people say how serene I seemed, how easy it was to be around me, how tranquil I appeared. That was not how I would have ever described myself then! It was not my inner experience, which I would have characterized back then as a Mexican jumping bean. *I was incongruent with my Energy Signature.* Through that basic disconnection, my body suffered as a result.

I only grew into my Signature through the development of a personal practice of being in the world and experimenting with the same system I'm sharing with you. So you'll have a variety of tools to ensure that the relationship with yourself, that most meaningful relationship you can ever have, will be a positive, nourishing one.

I own now that my slower movements, my direct slow gaze—my Energy Signature—are married to my identity. No longer am I striving to be bubbly, for example, something I tried and failed to be throughout my 20s. Through the Cranial Alchemy work I've synthesized and practice daily, I can't imagine being anyone other than the best version of me I can dream into being. Knowing this truth about myself can, in seconds, get me off any hamster wheel of disconnection and confusion and helps move me on to a productive path, a line of self-inquiry, whatever life throws my way. There is so much we can mine from our bodies.

Think about this remark from Gil Hedley, PhD, who teaches a unique layer by layer dissection class: "Your liver doesn't spend time thinking 'Maybe I should do what the gallbladder is doing.' It just does what a liver does. Nothing in nature wastes time wondering if it should be more like someone else."

The first step to success is knowing what energy is yours. The next step is knowing what is other.

Energy Exercise One

Some people, of course, and perhaps you're one of those people, aren't sure whether or not they feel energy. If while doing Bringing Down Heaven you felt like you were just waving your arms around ballet-style, try this: Rub your hands together with your palms flat for 30 seconds. Keep the palms pressed together when you stop rubbing. Then, slowly, begin to separate your palms.

Do you feel a fizzy connection as your palms move apart? Some people feel heat; some feel their hands "pulling" back together. Move your hands only as far away from each other as you can while *still* feeling that connection, however you're experiencing it.

This little exercise will give you an idea of how you feel energy and is a start to owning your own blueprint of sorts, your Energy Signature. If you were able to move your hands shoulder-width apart, for example, your Signature is likely robust and highly aware. If you kept your hands close together but felt the connection for a while before the connection dissipated, your Energy Signature may well be contained, private. Now, going through your senses, note if, as you rubbed hands together, you sensed a color, or if you associated a sound with the process. Take stock of what if any sense you had of a sensory shift. Would you say this felt calming or energizing? Play with this simple exercise and note any changes.

Another exercise (this one to try with a partner) is to determine whether your Signature routinely involves putting energy into another person or situation or pulling energy out.

We all have had the experience of watching someone enter a room and sucking all the air out of the place. Conversely, we've hopefully all had the experience of someone walking into a room and, by their simple presence, making everything seem sunnier.

Let's try this Craniosacral training exercise to ascertain where you fall in between those two extremes.

Energy Exercise Two

Sit comfortably in a chair, feet flat on the floor, your hands parallel to your thighs, hovering slightly above them. Your intention is to put

energy into your legs. Lower your hands until you feel an energetic connection. Use the least amount of pressure possible. Some people feel the
energy while their hands are still off-body.

Now, to pull energy out of your legs, start with your hands firmly
on your thighs. Begin to lift them, backing off the pressure just until
that moment when you are aware of the sensation that you're pulling your energy out. Look to see where your hands are when you no
longer feel any sensation lingering on your thighs. Remember, there
is no right or wrong. Some of you will feel the energy pulled away
when your hands are barely touching your thighs; others' hands may
be lifted several inches. Again, this offers you information as you collect the elements that comprise your Energy Signature. Note whether
you were more comfortable pulling energy out or putting energy in.
Your goal is to strike a balance for yourself and be consciously aware
of your energetic Signature.

Energy Exercise Three—You in Physical Relationship to Others

The next time you find yourself around a group of people—at your
office, in a meeting, on a bus, or at a family gathering—try this exercise.
See how close you can stand or sit next to someone before you sense
tension or before the other person engages you or asks you what you
want. This exercise will help you calibrate how your Energy Signature
works for or against you and will help you determine how to best connect in any given situation. Different cultures as well as individuals have
their own thresholds of awareness. I'm reminded of the "pushers" that
Japan's subways used to employ so that riders didn't have to apologize
for standing so close to strangers. In some eastern European countries,
yelling and talking have a thin line of demarcation, as does the idea of
personal space.

What may seem "too close for comfort" to someone you want to
communicate with might be no problem for you, but the exchange
won't go well unless you are able to adjust. In this case, you'd need to
pull back to allow the other person "some space." But first you must
have that awareness easily available to you.

For now, simply notice where you related comfortably and when your proximity to someone began to feel uncomfortable for either of you. Naturally, in attempting this, exercise common sense. Initially, you'll want to try this exercise with people you know.

Energy Exercise Four—You in Relationship to Place

Let's begin this exercise with what home is to you. First, on a piece of paper write out the physical qualities of what you think it is. Then, using all your senses, detail some of the components that add up to home— what you see, hear, smell, feel, and taste when you think of home.

My sense of home when I was young was wherever my mom was. Our family moved a lot, my father was largely absent, and I didn't associate home with bricks and mortar but rather with my mother and everything about her.

What is home to you? Dive into the exploration. Remember, be deliberate in your choice of words here and use all your senses, embellishing your description as specifically as you can.

Once you have your description of home, look back through your life to see if and when it changed for you. What was home to you when you were a child? A teenager? A young adult? Write down those changes.

For me, home changed from childhood to teen years and again after college when I lived in a tiny studio apartment on the East Side of Manhattan. This contrasted greatly with the modern Westside duplex I called home when I married. These days, home is suburban Los Angeles, and though my property is small by West Coast standards, as a former Manhattanite, my home energetically feels spacious.

If I were to work through this exercise now, I'd go back over these five home designations and write down the smells I remember from each. The sounds, for another example, are different from the East Side of Manhattan to the West Side of that same city. So even if you've lived in the same city your whole life, not only will your sense of awareness change, but your views can change on all three levels with which we're working.

After you have completed the exercise with home, do it again with one or two other places that hold significance for you. Use your felt sense as you choose. Which places call to you now? Which are resonant and hold significance for you inside your body?

Energy Exercise Five—You in Relationship to the World

"The world and I reciprocate one another."[4]—David Abram

How do you see, feel, and experience yourself in relationship to the world? I'm not talking about your family world or your work world. I'm talking about the whole wide world. Some people have never given much thought to this, but now is your chance to do so. Do you view the world as primarily benign? Perhaps you view it as a minefield? And where are you in that benign place or that minefield?

I invite you to describe for yourself your relationship to the world. At first, if you can, do this out loud. Notice if the sound, the tone of your description, is more "Wheeee" or more "Er, um." After you notice that, write down what you have just described out loud.

Next, ask how that relationship came to be. Do you like it? Are you resigned to it? Are you excited by it? Is it unclear to you?

Now, where do you feel all that in your body at this moment?

Exercise Six—Walking Energy Meditation

Here we're after a deepening, a connection you might have passed over, a resonance to be nurtured, a small noticing.

Pick a 20-minute period of daylight time during which you will not be interrupted. If possible, you're going to do this walking meditation three times during one week. This is a terrific way to begin experiencing how nature speaks to you through your body.

Pick three different places:

1. A city street environment.
2. An easy nature hike or beach walk.
3. Your neighborhood.

If there is crossover between any two of these three, pick three environments that vary as much as possible, with one having more concrete, one rich with natural beauty, and one a place you know like the back of your hand. I grew up in New York City, so my neighborhood was concrete and apartment-filled. However, if I did this exercise in New York today, I might pick my three different spots as Rockefeller Center, a small park area, and my Upper West side block—perhaps a walk to the corner newsstand. Now, because I live in Los Angeles, I might pick a Wilshire Boulevard office complex, a Santa Clarita horse barn, and a walk around my suburban cul-de-sac neighborhood.

Now, here's your task:

1. On your city walk, I want you to find untouched nature.
2. On your nature walk, I want you to find cutting edge connection or machine-made splendor.
3. On your familiar neighborhood walk, I want you to find something alien and wonderfully (or awfully) odd.

After each walk, come back home and jot down the three discoveries/presents. Make up a one paragraph (or so) story about how each discovery/present of yours came to be. Have fun with this. And save your stories. We'll revisit them later, in Chapter 8.

~ ~ ~

This essay is my costume designer last hurrah and combines my shifting values at that time with an internal gift that made me aware that what I value is the intangible, the metaphorical—which is available to us all when we practice observing. When you can smoothly switch from a physical to a metaphorical level, you will be able to release stress on the spot and sometimes, as you'll see in the following essay, you'll be able to see Wonderland in the unlikeliest places.

Essay: Super Thrift Store

On Saticoy near Woodman in deepest darkest Van Nuys, sits the Super Thrift Store. It is a dismal looking building, but it's a Hollywood costumer's secret garden. Due to the scavenger energy required to work through the racks of stuff, low-budget Hollywood usually finds its way here. Now times are tough again, and I'm swerving past the chain link fence into the blacktop parking lot, desperate. I am working on a comedy (I use that term loosely) about two blonde, sexy, large-busted girls who wear string bikinis all day long, every day, looking for Mr. Right. I don't think I have to worry about divulging any secrets because that could describe any of thousands of low budget films ever made. This one has a twist. But of course you knew that. I'll spare you the twist.

I have dragged Mimi here; she's new to film. For the last six years she has costumed a daytime show with label whore divas who need designer shoes even for those scenes in which there is no chance their feet will be shown on camera. I will bet anything she has never shopped at the Super Thrift Store, but Mimi is a sport.

To reach the entrance we must pass the drop-off point that is actually a super drop-off point, meaning that goods from over 10 smaller drop-off points wind up here, where they're sorted, and under some curious hierarchy, which tells me everything has an ego, the best stuff shines under florescent light strips next door at Super Thrift Store. The lesser garments one can only pray for. The proceeds from any purchases go to help families who can't help themselves. I never before knew exactly what "sundries" described, but now I have an understanding of that word because some of these sale items are indescribable. A cane missing a handle? Celine Dion room freshener? Oh, maybe that's perfume. Still.

Mimi and I race around, filling our cart with finds. Hip hop jeans, check! Oh, and there are some tangerine-colored Juicy flip flops with fake diamonds streaming from a baby pin—99 cents, check! Oh, and a short black skirt in a size zero—50 cents and fabulous. We can put that on the snooty lead and freak her out when she wants to buy it at the end of filming. That will be fun. Triples of a wrap-around pleated satin halter top—tags still attached. We know we will need triples for the jello scene. I said I would spare you the twists in this extravaganza, but there's one.

Piles and piles of stuff spill over the sides of our cart. Mimi says we have just 500 bucks. I know our stash will cost well under. At checkout, the reality of this place sinks in. Ahead of us is a mother with two young sons who want two toys that are out of their packages but still seem new. To these boys the toys spell the Promised Land. They show their mom the shiny water blasters, one lime green, the other slick black. The mom carefully looks them over. I know she is delaying disappointing her boys. She asks the clerk how much. Two dollars. Each. She tells the boys she can get them one. They have to choose. I want to pay this stranger's entire bill and buy those kids every toy on the shelf. But I know better than to make any grand gesture. What am I going to say? "Hello, idealistic baby boomer here, I have unresolved issues of lack and fairness and I'd like to project that onto your family?"

I have friends who grew up extremely poor but didn't know until high school that they were poor, and I know, no one has a right to mess with Mom's word, especially not a middle class white costumer who has 500 bucks to spend on stuff that may never be used. I begin to examine the ceiling tiles until they leave and it's our turn to tally.

Our haul totals $300. Mimi is impressed. We have covered several principal asses, I hope, and we wend our way back to the car, avoiding a potential trip over a group of kids' bikes lying on their sides waiting to see if they'll make the grade for Super Thrift Store or if they'll have to ride off into lesser sunsets.

We load the car as only professionals can, and discuss a potential Starbucks run. At the exit gate, a thin, middle-aged, dark-complexioned man in a washed out, beige button-down shirt and worn but well-pressed trousers, stops us. He is out of breath. He waves delicate arms above his head to get our attention. I am confused. I am in a rush. My internal dialog starts with "What's the deal, pal?" Out loud I call out the window, "Is there something wrong?" in the tone I have in the past reserved for that final classic, "Officer?"

The man looks intently at me. He runs his thin fingers through thinner hair. The air around us waits, suspended. Mimi waits. I wait. He looks at my Lexus as if to assure himself that I am the one he wants to speak with. "Excuse me, but you made a large purchase inside, just now, yes?"

"Uh, yeah." I am ready to floor the gas pedal and get out of there. This hold up has made Starbucks out of the question. I am thinking, "Spit it out, man. What on God's earth do you have to say?" Does he think our 100s are counterfeit?

"I am the manager here, of this store..."

My inner smart ass cramps. Speed it up man. What's the dealio? I am beside myself, hands on the wheel, ready to fly. Mimi gives me a dark look, or am I imagining that?

"Ladies I, well...God Bless You. This sale with us today, it means we can help so many this weekend. Ladies, if there's something...maybe something you had to leave behind today in the store?"

I do not know what to say to this guy. "Wow" comes to mind but that won't work.

He continues. "I would like to give you each a small thank you, sorry, a gift, yes, for this miracle. An item you wanted, maybe?"

I look at Mimi and feel tears start heating up inside. She is silent. I say, "Thank you so much, but we have to go now. We will be back." He looks sad so I add, "It's a generous offer, thank you," and he brightens.

He says, "Please, just remind me of this day if you come back, okay?"

"I will be back," I promise. "Thank you so much," I add, thinking of water blasters.

As we drive toward Burbank, I allow the wave I am feeling to slosh up inside. Manager man wanted to give me a gift. Did I leave something behind, he asked. Something I could not afford? Yes, I think, now fully aware of something I cannot afford to lose. A healthy dose of humanity. A paradigm shift I didn't know I needed.

"Can you believe that just happened, Mimi?"

"Yeah, I know. Forget Starbucks, huh?"

I can't tell with her what she's thinking, exactly.

I decide to keep my present close to my heart for as long as I can.

Recap of Chapter 3

Concepts

- ❀ Working with your luminous field of energy.
- ❀ Energy Signature.

Tools

- ❀ Bringing Down Heaven.
- ❀ Energy exercises.
- ❀ You in relationship to others, to place, to the world.
- ❀ Walking Meditation to shake things up.

Chapter 4

I Don't Kill Bugs

Our task must be to free ourselves...by widening our circle of compassion to embrace all living creatures and the whole of nature and its beauty.

—Albert Einstein

Lots of people talk to animals.... Not very many listen, though.... That's the problem.

—Benjamin Hoff, *The Tao of Pooh*

During a retreat I co-led in Joshua Tree, California, I worked hands-on with participants, outside, one-on-one, beneath a sheltered patio. The vast desert spread out before us, and there in the arid heat I worked six sessions in one day, something I rarely do. The only constant presence on that patio was me, but each time a woman lay down upon the table, a different animal came to the patio's edge, the spot where the patio met the desert floor. Three of those animals stand out for me.

Once a bird perched on the overhang throughout the hour and left as soon as the woman on the table opened her eyes.

Another woman had a snake quickly slither up toward the table; it came to a sudden stop and lightly placed his head on the concrete, silently watching her entire session.

Another woman had a fly buzz around her neck for the whole hour, and because I had been there all day I knew that no other flies had appeared that day! In cranial work, the neck is part of the Avenue of Expression, so the appearance of the fly gave us a chance to talk during the session about how she saw her ability to communicate and later to talk about her images of "flitting around" and "being annoying" and "feeling that everything was relentless."

Those visits were an unusual example of guides/Inner Wisdom actually showing up as outer wisdom. Each of those women had an opportunity to look inside and see what *bird, snake,* and *fly* meant to her and how those totems might be operating in their individual lives. Seeing the animals as Inner Wisdom gave each woman a specific perspective that allowed her to make a deeper internal connection.

Like the women who were able to shift their understanding thanks to these unexpected visitors, the notion here is that it is important to remain wholly aware and to allow yourself to have shifts in perspective. Normally, most of us are not programmed to do this. We usually put on our blinders and follow a straight path, keeping armor on to protect ourselves at all costs from unforeseen forces. Unfortunately, we do this at the expense of our imagination and creative emergence. Working with animals, being aware of the "fly" in your ointment, can swiftly move you from stuck to unstuck.

When you develop the new habit of seeing your body as a whole, connected to all you have ever experienced and all you are experiencing now, when you learn to view your body as a wise ally whose tissues can reveal patterns that are not serving you in your life now, then you can experience real freedom of choice to change what you want to change on a molecular level. When you learn to fully soak in your positive, fully engaged life experiences, your molecules have no choice but to shift.

It is healing to be in conscious relationship to all your animal encounters.

Look in the Direction You Want the Horse to Go

Some years ago I participated in a women's empowerment day at a Malibu horse ranch. My experience there was a disaster, largely due to my expectations that we'd be working energetically with the horses and my disappointment when that did not happen. Still, I did learn that if you want a horse to move, it's good to look in the direction you want the horse to go. Some days after the workshop, it occurred to me that, metaphorically speaking, those are words to live by. In other words, it's important not to stare at your past while attempting to create your next move forward. Don't plead with a horse who doesn't know what you want him to do while facing in the direction opposite to where you want him to move.

Sound confusing? Imagine the horse's confusion.

More recently, Sara Fancy of the Silver Horse Healing Ranch began to teach me how to engage with horses energetically. This natural horsemanship work goes beyond the work I already practice—the Upledger Equine Craniosacral method of connecting to horses. Sara's herd is teaching me expansion with economy of motion. Again, this is an example of a streamlined elegance to working in concert with nature.

My Cranial Alchemy work dovetails with Sara's teachings, and her horses are the most no-nonsense energy teachers I've had. Horses quickly show you their Energy Signature, and they also decide about you quickly. They are masters at conserving energy, a skill most of us humans could benefit from adopting. Using the nature-based exercises you've practiced thus far, you'll become adept at tracking your energy expenditure, and working with animals is a great way to test the limits of your Energy Signature. Doing so enables awareness as to whether or not your Energy Signature works in concert with nature or requires fine tuning.

As an example: During one session at Sara's ranch I was in the round pen with Jackie, the second lead mare of Sara's herd. As I walked Jackie around in a circle, with a bridle and loose lead only, she tested me when I signaled her to stop with my body language but she did not stop cleanly. As I looked for ways to connect with this beautiful, highly sensitive Appaloosa/Belgian cross, I had to reassess my intention. During our walk, we were stopping arbitrarily as an exercise, and I admit, my intention was muddy. I realized that I had no real investment in stopping and my lack of investment was reflected back, through the horse, immediately. Why should she exert energy following my instructions if even I wasn't fully invested in those instructions? She "read" my body's muddy intention energetically. And so, I checked in with my central nervous system, my RAS, by placing a hand on my chest and locating some internal stillness. Then I resumed walking alongside Jackie. I opened my senses to keep myself in the present moment with no expectations.

The instant my perspective widened and I tuned in sensorily, I became aware of the sound of her stride, the clop-clop musicality of it. I matched the sound of her steps with my own—not the length of her stride, which I couldn't have easily kept up with, but the sound, the percussion of it. It became our shared and steady language, a connection I had previously overlooked. And then everything changed. When I wanted her to stop, she stopped smoothly.

This is one explanation of why I ask clients questions to deepen their connection to their senses. In this instance, my connection to the mare came via my auditory awareness and my creative openness. (In Chapter 6 we'll talk about styles of relationship, one of which is mirroring, and in Chapter 7 we'll cover the role of music and sound in healing.) In this instance, I was mirroring a repetitive sound of Jackie's as my way into a deeper connection with her. As a sensitive horse will usually do, she then "tuned" into us as a team and we completed our exercises seamlessly, in synchrony.

Drawing an unbridled horse into you energetically is a deeper layer of interaction involving an energetic invitation while at the same time putting no pressure on the horse. This was another crucial lesson I learned from Sara and her herd. She reminded the class of the similarity in this instance to waiting for an important phone call. When you obsessively stare and fiddle with your phone, it rarely rings. Put your focus elsewhere, no longer invested in the outcome, and the phone often rings. This notion is the Pressure/No Pressure concept. This works as well with humans as it does for four-legged creatures. In the natural world, a direct gaze, even if it's soft, signifies pressure. In some cultures it might signify a challenge, but even if it does not, it does indicate a kind of demand. Just the act of offering someone a direct gaze has the effect of pressuring, even if you don't consciously feel you're demanding anything. The frequency of a direct front facing gaze speaks for you. For the horse, such a gaze would elicit the question: "What does she want from me?"

But without a clear request, a direct gaze offers a mixed message. You want something but the horse is not sure what. The result is likely that the horse will do nothing. Take the pressure off by turning your attention toward something or someone else, and the horse now has options. With no pressure, movement becomes more likely. Movement in relationship toward you becomes possible. A client recently blurted out after the Pressure/No Pressure explanation: "Jeannine, that's just like dating!"

Practicing this process, I was given the length of a popular song to enter the arena with one of Sara's geldings, a 30-year-old Arabian named Silver. I'd worked with Silver before and had discovered his goofy, hammy side. I hoped to connect again in that same way. But that in and of itself was an expectation, and as I've said, expectations don't fuel the natural world or foster relationship to it.

With Silver I had a pre-thought-out plan and a desire, which, to a certain degree, left Silver and the present moment out of the equation. What would intrigue Silver enough to inspire him to approach me that day? During the entire five-minute song, he did not come near. This time I got his interest but was unable to lure him to me until the very last seconds when I turned to exit the arena. Again, this offered a lesson about staying in the moment and working with what *is* instead of what we wish or think should be.

You may try adding Pressure/No Pressure to your experiment of You in Relationship to Others from Chapter 3. Note the shifts.

Horses are healing. Their luminous field is huge—some say 10 times larger than a human's luminous field. That may explain why equine programs for autistic children as well as for prison inmates have been successful as rehabilitation vehicles. I know horse people who say that spending one half hour with a horse can be the equivalent to 10 hours of talk therapy. They have a point. If you are lucky enough to live around horses or to have access to energetically interact with them, I recommend it. If you are afraid of horses, I invite you to do some Inner Reconnaissance around that fear. Ultimately, you'll learn more about your styles of relationship, especially if you practice being in the present moment via your senses. Of course, working with dogs, cats, and birds can feed your soul and help the healing process as well. However, the larger the animal, the more immediately obvious the connection or disconnection is, oftentimes with higher stakes. The larger the luminous energy field of the animal, the larger the encompassing healing potential.

The classes with Sara reminded me of a prior horse experience with an emphasis on the human rapport. This experience describes, in another scenario, the clarity we can gain from being open to what is right in front of us.

Twenty years before that first day at Sara's ranch, I took a horse-packing, eco-friendly trip with my then-husband, Phil. Two months earlier I had had abdominal surgery, and my New York City born-and-bred husband had never been on a horse. Our trip was taking us to Yellowstone where we would trace the path of the Nez Perce Native Americans, but I worried that neither of us was as steady as horse people must be. I worried especially that Phil would feel uneasy because I had had some experience with horses when I was a child. Throughout the 10-day trip, the weather was rainy, and recent fires had blackened the hills. Still, as the 12 of us, along with our grizzled Nez Perce leader and his cowboy assistant, traveled through this magical land, I felt as if I were in a dream come true.

I didn't broadcast my recent surgery. I allowed Phil to carry my pack and endured everyone's teasing me about that. I still dug a latrine and held my own in terms of chores, but the first night it began to pour. We raised our tent and waited for dinner—a long wait. At some point, Phil went to see if he could help the cowboys, and he showed this grizzled Nez Perce buff how covering a grill pan can hasten the cooking process. That night, thanks to Phil, dinner was saved. After that, despite Phil's lack of horsemanship, our cowboys treated him with deference. They gave him tips on working the reins. A trip that might have been awful for Phil turned out to be remarkable.

What amazed me beyond that simple yet dinner-saving tip was watching that moment when, in an instant, Phil's feeling of separateness vanished. Of course, such opportunities are most available if you're grounded enough to catch them. Phil might not have tried to help the cowboys, but he comes from a restaurant family, and even out there in the wilderness, he discovered the grounded corner of his expertise. In the most unlikely circumstance, he became a hero.

There are, of course, divides that cannot be bridged. One traveler, Jack, was a young single man from China, on the trip to see the "old west" and to learn about the Nez Perce. He wore Vegas-style western clothing instead of Levis and worn flannels. He asked to be photographed with each of the single women in our group. As the trip progressed, he became more and more dejected. I thought his demeanor might have been due to the available women's lack of interest in his advances, but midweek during a group after-dinner fire, when we had to camp without crossing a creek our itinerary indicated we were scheduled to cross, he became indignant.

"Why are we not on the other side of the creek as our paperwork indicates we should be?" was his first question.

The slow answer came back: "Jack, the river has risen with all the rain and the horses can't cross." Jack wanted to know what he was missing on the other side and demanded to know whether there would be a partial refund.

From there the true source of his dejection emerged. "Where are the landmarks?" he demanded. "Where did Chief Joseph give his speeches? Where did he travel—there are no markers!"

I watched him and thought silently that he needed to find Native American Disneyland where even the photo opportunities would be marked. But as I sat there watching and listening, I began to reconsider my dismissal of his concerns.

Jack had a linear perspective as to what was possible on a horse-packing trip. He hadn't grown up learning Native American lore. Although I was content to know we were in proximity to the spot where the tribe had traveled, and though my imagination was enough for me and the other travelers, Jack thought differently—he had no images from his past to attach to what we were seeing, where we were traveling.

One night a buffalo had walked right past our tent, but did I need to know more about that buffalo? No. Rather, my imagination allowed me to envision many more buffalo roaming the Nez Perce land. Also, since I came from Manhattan, I loved the fact that our itinerary had changed because of something as natural as rising waters—the kind of thing that seldom changes life in a city. Indeed, that was a feature I might have paid extra for.

In retrospect, it turns out that night was my awareness of what I would later understand is an essential Craniosacral concept: the Direction of Ease, the idea that moving in the direction that's easier will ultimately allow movement in the other, more challenging direction. That night the river rising was an old west experience more real than anything on our itinerary. Those of us able to allow the non-linear into our perception were joyful, whereas Jack, fighting against that idea, was miserable.

And so, how might Jack have learned to move in the Direction of Ease? And how might you? The Transformation Circle work described in this chapter can help you to allow a deepening of consciousness, an allowing. Maybe you have an illness. Maybe you can't cross the river. Now what?

People who work closely with nature and with animals have to be steady or a 1,500-pound animal will make the decision of what to do for them. Sometimes we have 1,500 pounds of old stories making our decisions for us. What if, instead, we simply let the river rise? You haven't any choice about it anyway.

Jack was disappointed there were no specific spots where events had occurred and didn't understand the concept of western lore. Because he hailed from another culture entirely, he had an excuse.

This trip was one of my favorites, though it's also true that during that one week I moved from loving it to hating it and back again several times—this is because I allowed the experience simply to be. I couldn't control it and I didn't try, and it unfolded for me a new view of my husband, of cultural differences and, yes, of Chief Joseph's wisdom, as well as my healing body's wisdom. This valuable ability to learn to creatively notice does take time and focus, but it can be yours, with help from the following transformative Circle tool.

The Transformation Circle Tool

This is a fun and profound tool to reconnect you to your body so you can access your hidden inner resources. It's a key inside yourself.

In time, you'll relate to these Circle elements on all three levels:

The physical, which is apparent, is the daily flesh we live in. Aches, pains, dis-ease, hot/cold. This level also houses our superficial presentation of who we are. We're after illustrating our Circle beyond this level. But it's a starting place. At this level clients often use their string and stones to illustrate their face or abdomen.

The metaphysical level encompasses the mental, our ability to grasp ideas. It begins to work with the power of the unseen. At this level, clients will add in an illustration of their thoughts and feelings.

The metaphorical level is art, stories, music, and creating from abundance and childlike joy. At this level, anything is possible and linear connections make way for a suspended state of significance to the body, a stillness, at which point you'll sometimes feel as if your hands are choosing elements for your Circle of their own accord.

Your Transformation Circle can work on all these levels, depending on you and your willingness to step outside the box (and into the Circle). Through time, the Transformation Circle is especially helpful in attuning you to the soulful metaphorical level. That is why it's comprised of beauty, nature, and sacred components. And it's fun.

This Circle will be an inexpensive, unique tool using natural elements and found objects to create a space for a daily self-help artistic practice. Using the Circle, you begin to illustrate your inner life, your pain, or worries so you can discover and allow the shifts you need to change your circumstances.

You'll connect with your Inner Compass, in a visual and tactile way.

Using the Transformational Circle as a tool, an extension of your Inner Compass, you are experimenting and illuminating physical ailments, feelings, relationships, and default worldviews.

Creating Your Transformation Circle

Here is what you need to create your own starter Circle kit:

An 18×18 piece of medium to heavy weight fabric. Textured is best, and a light, neutral color is preferable. You'll see why as you start working with the various elements you'll collect and add to your kit. I like monk's cloth or burlap which is inexpensive at fabric shops.

A type of string. You can use colored string or a string of beads or a leather strip or even a long shoelace. I like seed beads or rudraksha beads and I also keep a selection of chakra-colored satin string so I can use the colors I'm drawn to each time I use my Transformation Circle.

You might also choose to use a mala or a favorite necklace as your Circle. In Cranial Alchemy work we meet the client "where they are." As you meet yourself in this new way, use what you have, start with where you are.

Now you can be on the lookout for natural items and you can also include special items that have meaning to you, such as an old locket, charm, or a coin, perhaps.

I collect turtle totems so in my Transformation Circle kit I have several. One is a small turtle carved out of bone. I don't often use it in my daily Circle, but it's a personal reference that serves to focus me inward each morning. These kinds of items I keep in a separate corner of the fabric square, in a small tray or bowl, outside of the Circle.

Here's a Circle of mine, created using a mala of rudraksha beads and two of my turtles. This represented how deeply supported and uplifted I felt when my friend Evelyn helped me unexpectedly one day. I wanted to anchor that feeling of fortunate assistance. Metaphorically, a feather and the butterflies felt nourishing and airy to include in my Circle. The turtles are holding space, focused on the center (Figure 4-1 on page 103).

Play with the process of collecting feathers, stones, twigs, acorns, seeds, and shells for your kit.

Figure 4-1

You may want to collect leaves. Go out for a walk, and look anywhere but straight ahead (of course you will need to from time to time).

Imagine you're a bird building a nest—what looks like good nest material? Perhaps try walking a block or two with that as your intention.

Now shift your focus from a bird's needs to what you as a human find pleasing in nature. What will resonate for your Circle? Allow fascination with the smallest offering from nature. When those offerings show themselves, allow them to seep into your awareness.

Here's a story about how I found a special feather for my kit. Dr. Diane Sandler, founder of Cellular Yoga, has been both a friend and a mentor of mine for many years. She has three gorgeous birds, two are macaws, and their feathers are brilliant. She gifted me with long tail feathers they had shed. They were vermillion and electric blue with a green backing, and I was overcome with their beauty.

I knew the personalities of these birds and that imbued each set of feathers with meaning. The blue and gold ones came from a bird that represents bravery and survival. She says when she's lonely, "Don't you want a bird? I'm a good bird." Now I know that someone will say, "Oh, someone taught her to say that in a pet shop." But this bird is well loved and has had her home for a long time and the *only* time she says this is when her owners are busy and don't have time for her. Pretty smart communication, I think!

I think of these feathers as wise and loving.

The other bird is more playful. I instinctively use one of his feathers in my Circle on days when I need to imbue a little mischief into the concern I bring to my Circle.

Do I do this consciously? Not really, but as you get into in the flow of working with your Circle, you might. Eventually, your intuition will take over. You're flexing that intuition muscle in this practice, strengthening it.

So far I've mentioned flashy, gorgeous feathers. But a month ago, I stepped out onto my back patio and looked down at a single, tiny dove grey feather just lying on the brick. There was nothing else around and I walked about my yard looking for another sign of the bird or other fallen feathers. No sign.

I added the feather to my Circle kit and, though it was nowhere as beautiful as the macaw feathers, it had arrived in a most magical, surprising way and I was grateful. A small law of attraction in motion moment!

Before I started my Circle work, I would not have noticed that single small grey dove's feather. I would have walked right by it—feathers were not on my radar, not in my perceptual field. Not even if they were placed right in my path. But I had a rich moment of gratitude and magic because of that feather just outside my door.

Think what small wonder is waiting for you to notice it. Imagine if you could fold that into your urban day and allow it to move you internally toward ease.

If you decide to incorporate Transformation Circle work into your hectic day, each day you'll see how your body starts to mirror wonder and nature so you can heal and feel nurtured by the world around you. Doesn't that sound nourishing compared to solely behaving as though you're a warrior in a battlefield of traffic, meetings, stressful relationships, and work?

Your perceptual hunt might yield natural treasures closer than you know. So this exercise is like dropping a pebble into a pond and seeing the circles it creates that ripple ever outward.

Focus back to your Circle crafting.

As you are on the collecting path, you are looking for elements of nature and found objects that "speak" to you. When you've gathered a selection, group them by what element they belong to, water, earth, sky, or found treasure.

I have pockets sewn into my kit so I keep each group together and ready to go to work for me. For example, sky elements might fit well in one of the upper corners; earth, one of the lower corners.

Now, take the piece of string and create your Circle for the day. Leave it empty as you close your eyes.

Next, easily scan your body and pick the issue you want to work with today or allow it to surface for you if you're comfortable with the process.

Take a minute or two scanning, allowing, with eyes still closed. Then when ready, open your eyes and look at your Circle. What needs to be there inside it to illustrate your issue? Use your soft eyes of wonder, and look around your Circle at all the tools of nature, gifts you have available.

Trust that after a few times working with your Circle, you'll find your hands instinctively reaching for what belongs inside it that day. But give that time and know that there's nothing wrong with choosing consciously for as long as it takes you to trust and allow the bubbling up to take over.

Know that on any given day, you may have 10 items in your Circle or one. Now go about your day. At the end of the day, revisit what you created in the morning. Ask yourself: What's changed? If it's still the same, how does each element make you feel?

If a shift has taken place, how would you illustrate that in your Circle now? Play with it for a few minutes and then wipe the slate clean. Put your tools away. Plan to do it again in the morning.

Consistency is key. Noticing your resistance is also important as is marking your shifts as they occur.

In private workshops, I often bring along all the Transformation Circle ingredients so participants work with my stash of shells, feathers, sticks, stones, and found objects. Begin your own stash with what you find during your walks from Chapter 3.

Using Your Transformation Circle Through Time

Create your Circle daily, twice a day, and the path to transformation, shift, and clarity follows. The practice takes less than eight minutes twice a day.

What shifts might you expect?

For everyone: Shift your perception of your issue so you become open and aware of out-of-the-box solutions. For anatomy geeks: Create a relationship between your limbic system and your neocortex so you have balance in your brain. For creative artists: Access your imagination. It may even be your inspiration!

Accessing inspiration can be tricky, so begin with taking a scan of your daily habits. What do you absolutely do each day no matter what?

Remember, no one is going to read this and grade you if you rarely eat a nutritious breakfast, for example. So answer truthfully, and looking at your absolutes, ask this big question:

How many of those absolutes involve integrating your mind and your body?

For many people, our habits access either/or. Watching the news on the treadmill doesn't count. Neither does driving to work on autopilot!

Adding the Transformation Circle to your day can help you feel connected from the inside out. That's a great ability to have because it gives you access to fully participate in right now, rather than walling off feelings or pain in order to allow you to merely power through the day.

Right now is where you create from. Creating at the metaphorical level is the process that connects you so you can author and track your own life. When you begin to recognize what your Internal Compass is telling you, subtly and not so subtly, you're on the road to living in concert with all aspects of yourself. This includes what you like, what you don't, what you want to change, what you're afraid of, and even your discarded dreams.

This state gives you power so you can:

❀ Release your stress and pain.

❀ Reconnect with your body so you can have more access to your hidden inner resources.

❀ Imagine the life you want and the way you'd like to feel. Imagine being able to relate to your body on a regular basis with grace and ease.

❀ Visualize how you move in an integrated body, how getting up in the morning is a luxurious stretch to the sky and each formerly mundane task becomes fun and an act of presence.

❀ See yourself easily navigating your perfect day. Are you moving in the Direction of Ease now, even when faced with stress?

Practice Transformation Circle for these 30 days and your receptors will be tuned. Though you might not even fathom what feeling ease in the face of stress could possibly be, feel like, or look like, a shift will happen. Let's say your issue is that you tend to eat distractedly when stressed and you pay for it every afternoon.

Tomorrow you might choose to use your Transformation in this way: illustrate your "gut" in your Transformation Circle, imaging your gut filled with dark stones, for example, and perhaps realizing that there are no feathers in your gut, no lightness. This Transformation Circle can then be a visual Touchstone throughout your day.

Following the gut example, how might you "do" your day more deliberately to incorporate "lightness"? As you leave for lunch, this question takes a minute to ask and answer. If you get into this habit of asking, you're more likely to have shifted your Circle at the end of the day when it's time to do round two.

Here's how one private coaching client illustrated her brain (Figure 4-2). As you can see, at this time her cerebellum (base of skull) was feeling prickly and weighed down. By creating and working with a Transformation Circle, she was able to get out of her own way, access a different part of her brain, and clarify her pain—her feelings—by illustrating where she needed attention, in order to create a specific shift.

Figure 4-2

By making a Transformation Circle and using it as a tool, an everyday practice you can start shifts in your world and you'll "see" your issues differently than you do currently.

Think how freeing it would feel to have choices and a sense of ease when faced with stressful decisions and pain, to be able to get off the hamster wheel of fearful "what ifs" and to trust your gut.

Working with the Circle takes you "out of yourself" literally and figuratively. It's a "canvas" with objects from nature mirroring your internal state. You follow what shifts inside during your day, mark and acknowledge your state of body and state of mind, and note what does not shift.

The following are two photos illustrating a "Before" and "After" from one workshop participant (Figure 4-3, "Before" above Figure 4-4, "After"). Notice that one is not necessarily better than the other, but merely that they are vivid illustrations of how that participant felt when she arrived to the workshop and her inner state at the end of the first day. She didn't want to make a Circle for the before shot. You can see that, instead, she used her

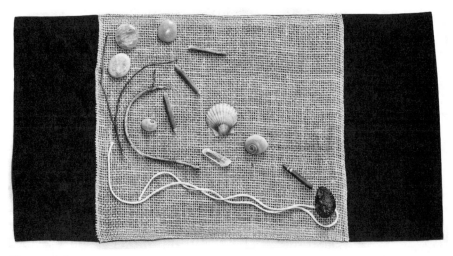

Figure 4-3

Figure 4-4

string to create a wavy line. Her elements were many and skewed to the one side. She reported to the group that she felt out of balance—that is what bubbled up for her after the group Inner Reconnaissance meditation.

For her after photo you may notice greater serenity. She removed several elements and created stepping stones on the lower right, as she described it, "to enter my circle with ease." Again, what matters here is what matters to the creator. Though I personally find beauty in all the before and after photos I've witnessed, sometimes the after doesn't change; sometimes the visual alteration is slight. The creative noticing and connection can be healing regardless of how many elements you use, how they look, and whether the change during your day is a radical revamp or a removal of one feather.

It's up to you how you use it, but if each time you approach both the making of it and the practice of it with a beginner's fresh eyes, you'll develop a relationship with your Inner Compass that many folks never do. And there's creative power and creative relief available to you in that Inner Compass relationship!

Figure 4-5, Love, is a literal but heartfelt Transformation Circle by a workshop participant illustrating how she felt at workshop's end. She used her Circle string in the "o" of the word, Love. May it inspire you as you create your own.

Figure 4-5

~~~

The following essay incorporates working Craniosacrally with a horse, and Direction of Ease, Inner Wisdom, and leaps on all Three Awareness Levels that we are working with in this book.

Essay: From Tolstoy to Degas in Orange County

I'm perched on the metal fence of a riding ring, in Silverado, California, staring at a thoroughbred named Degas. I'm studying an energy-based modality developed by Dr. John Upledger in the 1970s. It's called Craniosacral Therapy, and it worked so well on my endometriosis years ago that I took a class to find out more about it, then another class. Now I'm pushing 50 and have completely changed careers, from television costume designer to Craniosacral Therapist. But I have never before worked with animals.

Gail Wetzler, P.T., teacher of our group of 10 bodywork therapists, has chosen horses at this barn for us to work on. Degas has been chosen because none of the veterinarians can figure out why he won't jump for his owner. The owner is thinking of getting rid of him if he won't.

Degas is 15 years old, around 16 hands, and as I watch him in the ring, he seems impatient. I wonder if he has any idea that his fate might take a quick twist if this therapeutic effort doesn't help. He's watching us, waiting, one ear cocked, his right hoof raised with only the tip on the ground, as though en pointe.

This afternoon we will be using several techniques on Degas. Rock and glide, for example, is a way of gently nudging free restrictions found up and down the spine. Craniosacral techniques can also address emotional constrictions that present as physical issues. This week, 10 of us are here to learn to apply this body/mind modality to horses.

We form a loose circle around Degas. All of us are focused on Gail Wetzler, a thin, intense, physical therapist and Craniosacral teacher with piercing eyes and a no-nonsense history of working with high performance horses and impossible diagnoses. Her teaching assistant, Sally, demonstrates hand positions in the air, showing how to modify Craniosacral protocol for horses. We will use multiple hands on Degas to assess his condition.

I am new to this and nervous; suddenly I begin to think how funny it is that the term *hands* describes the height of a horse and now we are going to use our hands to keep him tall. Well, maybe it's not that funny.

Changing careers midlife was an enormous leap of faith. I haven't always seized chances that come my way, but I have always had sensitive hands, have been tactile in a detailed way. I don't fully understand what I'm doing in Silverado, but maybe I don't have to.

It is true that 30 years ago for one year on Broadway, I danced the role of a horse in a play with music based on a short story by Tolstoy. This, I think, is my link. To prepare for the part, I had to closely study horses. I am good at observing them, so maybe I can use what I know to find my way into Degas' cranial rhythm and palpate my way down his spine. Advanced therapists encourage neophytes to use what they know. And how many therapists have portrayed a Tolstoy horse on Broadway?

As one of the original cast of Tolstoy's *Strider: The Story of a Horse,* one minute I was toiling Off Broadway, and the next minute I was toasting our Broadway debut with a thin vial of chilled vodka at the Russian Tea Room. In the play, we dancers portrayed both horses and people, which may be why the moment I saw Degas, I wondered whether he understood the importance of this session. Was he aware that his fate was not his own to decide?

Strider follows the life and tragic death of a piebald horse. In his youth, he is torn from his mother and sent to auction where his life will either be saved or he will become horsemeat. At auction, he snags the attention of a prince.

At the time, I related to the role of the young damsel and the filly being wooed by three males—Darling, the perfect thoroughbred whose alter ego was a handsome Count; the Prince, who represented Imperial Russia; and Strider, the outcast.

Strider, born with piebald markings not superficially suited for a great lineage of horses, was the shunned outsider, but he dreamed big. He exhibited none of the Russian gloom and lingering question marks about the purpose of life. He had an altered perspective and here in Silverado 35 years later, so do I. Circling Degas, I relate less to the damsel than I do to Strider.

In the play, there is a split second when the Count tosses a rose to the damsel, but Strider catches it in his mouth, walks to the stands, bows on his hindquarters, and presents the rose to her. He inspires laughter in the powerful Prince who buys him to annoy the Count. Strider becomes the Prince's favorite horse.

Now, 10 pairs of open hands have a chance to change Degas' life course. I stand beside my colleagues and hear my intuition which sometimes speaks so clearly to me. My hands on his flank blend and meld with Degas' Inner Wisdom. As a dancer, I would have been catching the rose; as a healer, I am the one offering it. Under my hands, I feel Degas' body offer up a therapeutic pulse. I mentally image my way through the emotionally charged superficial fascia to feel the play between it and the deep fascia. What is each tuned to? I layer my awareness down to the organs, to the heart. What trapped energy is held there?

Thirty five years ago, I thought I understood the darkness of the play and its politics, but now, recalled from the flank of a horse, the story sparks something different in me. How many chances do we get? Is everything predestined so we might as well down that vodka and write poetry or go quietly mad? Can we reconcile politics with humanity? I feel the urge to cast the Food and Drug Administration as Imperial Russia—imperious and cloaked in authority.

Whoa, I tell myself; I am getting carried away. I need to sit; my arms are going numb. But Degas is in healing mode, his body working hard to unravel restrictions.

I add another five grams of pressure to the black flank and continue to blend and meld with this powerful horse. Waves of energy that I can only call sadness rush from his body. I have learned to trust my hands and to allow the client's body to let me know what it needs. The questions disappear; Tolstoy floats away as Degas' Inner Wisdom takes center stage. Degas won't jump. The vets say there is nothing physically wrong with him. How will we explain a horse's sorrow to an owner who wants only a jumping machine?

Alternative therapists are not branded piebald, but we might as well be. We reveal ourselves as unique health facilitators to a society that seeks double blind studies. Still, more and more people are turning to alternative care because the way we facilitate healing offers an investigation of the whole body, and we all live in our whole bodies, not in individual parts.

Degas takes a step back and drops his head. All 10 of us move soundlessly in sync with him. We are all in tune with his cranial rhythm and with each other. Degas goes into what in cranial work is called a Stillpoint, a divine space, a therapist-assisted pause in the Craniosacral system of the body that allows for self healing. I feel a palpable shift in the air around us. We are all exactly where we are supposed to be, and we all feel it for one elongated, elegant second.

Here I am in Orange County, piebald instead of a damsel, owning my calling, standing in the grace of Degas who is now very still, intent on the feel of a facilitating miracle, 10 pairs of hands on his 16. There's hope. There's hope all around.

I never got to see Degas jump, but in my mind's eye I see us taking our separate leaps, both of us landing with ease.

Recap of Chapter 4

Concepts

❀ Working with animals both physically and metaphorically.
❀ Pressure/No pressure.

Tools

❀ Transformation Circle. Though these circles are only one of the tools I use with clients in workshops and custom programs, after working with it for a while, most discover that the Circle itself takes on a Touchstone quality.

Definitions

Avenue of Expression—the Upledger Craniosacral name for the area comprising soft tissues just below the clavicles of the neck, up through the neck and the cranial nerves through the throat and up to and including the mouth and lips.

Rock and Glide—Upledger term for gentle intentioning of the cerebrospinal fluid up and down the spine; imagine energetic vertebral flossing.

Week 3

Navigating Levels
and
Tracking Neutral

Chapter 5

A Different Kind of Alteration

The things that give most of you the most grief are those things that initially you had a feeling response about, but then you talked yourself out of it for one reason or another.

—Abraham/Esther Hicks

I rely far more on gut instinct than researching huge amounts of statistics.

—Sir Richard Branson

In utilizing and creating your new habits with this book's natural tools and exercises, you'll find the signals from your gut are some of the most authentic to listen to and focus on. This is especially important for those of you who self-identify as making most of your decisions from the neck up. For those who are certain their best decisions come only from their brain, here is big news.

You have a second brain. Most people don't know that, but your second (enteric) brain is your gut. Whereas every other part of your body answers to the big boss, neocortex, the enteric brain operates as a rogue operative, living by its own rules and flying under the radar. Your second brain will, however, make itself known on an as-needed basis—whether it's occasional digestive distress or a chronic condition, your gut communicates directly with you. This chapter provides exercises for discovering, working with, and better understanding your gut connections.

Think about the last time a food made you feel unwell. How did you respond? If you popped a pill to allow yourself to continue to eat that food, think of what you were doing to your body by overriding your enteric brain. It's the utmost in self-disrespect.

Gut Exercise: Part One

Take a field trip to the grocery store, without a shopping list. Do bring a small notebook. Search out the food that is closest to its natural state. It's usually found on the store's perimeter.

In the produce section, your task is to stand still and survey the produce. See what attracts you and why. Just visually take it in and follow your eyes to what looks good. Is it something familiar? Are you attracted more to color or shape? Something you've never tried? Don't judge and don't worry that you might be blocking the aisle or that someone may think you're nuts. Nuts are not in the produce section.

Try smelling the fruit. Really take the time to have sensory experiences choosing what you are going to put in your gut. Do an olfactory inventory of the items you pass as you move down the aisles. Notice your inner monologue. The first time I did this I noticed rutabagas and jotted down in my notebook, "poor things." It didn't make sense, but I've learned to follow these non-linear connective tracks, and sure enough, when I asked my Inner Wisdom what that referred to, what seemed to bubble up "out of nowhere" but in fact came out of my cellular memory, was surprising. My maternal grandfather popped into my awareness. All I know about that side of the family is that they were Irish potato farmers. I don't self-identify with potato farmers, but that day I spent an appreciative 15 minutes in the root vegetable section of the grocery store. We'll talk more about ancestors and their role in relationship to your body in Chapter 6, but for now let's get back to your grocery store trip.

Listen for the signals and impulses you get. "Ooh, that smells yummy and citrus-y" or "Hmm, that's making me feel itchy."

You don't need to know in your big boss brain why you are responding the way you are, you just need to trust your gut. (Ahem.)

Gut Exercise: Part Two

Next, go to the Farmers' Market or an outdoor market and try the same exercise. Are you attracted to different foods here than you were in the grocery store? Jot down any sensory differences you notice. Go beyond the obvious.

The Orange Exercise

This exercise involves another layer of noticing. I offer this experience to workshop groups, but it also works well as a solo exercise. After you've tried it yourself, you might want to invite some friends over and experience the way the dynamics of the exercise change in a group.

You'll need five or six oranges in a bowl. You'll also need a notebook and pen.

Choose one orange from the bowl and put the bowl off to the side. Now you're going to spend some quality time with your orange. If you have a timer, set it for six minutes.

During your six minutes together, you can do anything except eat the orange. Begin the exercise by closing your eyes and tracing the skin with your fingers. Hold it in one hand and feel the weight of your orange.

Open your eyes. Check for blemishes. How do you imagine your orange received its scars? Was it carefully plucked from a tree or did it fall? Jot down your impressions.

Smell your orange. Use sensory words to describe the scent. If you need help with words, there's a jumpstart list in Chapter 8. Is your orange more oval in shape or round? Thin or thick-skinned? Is it a juice orange or an orange meant to be peeled?

Now, using your gut awareness, imagine you can see the energy field of this piece of fruit. Stay with this; there is no wrong way to do this exercise. Write down a sensory description of that surrounding field.

Imagine you had to describe your orange to a space alien who had never seen one. Write down your description.

With your remaining time, write the "Life of Orange" as you imagine your orange would tell the tale to oranges back home, those still on the tree.

Now bring the bowl with the other oranges back in front of you and close your eyes. Place your orange in the bowl and with your eyes remaining closed, jumble up the oranges. Spin the bowl slowly. Stop. Open your eyes. Can you find your orange? How do you know for certain you have? Is the recognition a feeling, an inner knowing, or is it a physical clue that has informed you? Or, if you can't find it, can you narrow down the choices? Notice the senses with which you lead in this quest.

I've seen people in workshops get quite proprietary about claiming their orange once they realize they have to identify it. They'll rush up to the bowl with admirable concentration. Suddenly an everyday piece of fruit has meaning. It moves from ordinary to extraordinary. It's your personal orange; you've seen its value on a new level. This type of inquiry also works well with stones, flowers, and truly any element that you encounter in your day. Zero in on a few this week. Be certain they're elements you currently view as ordinary.

Whereas the value of this exercise lies not in whether or not you feel proprietary toward your orange, the skill you want to cultivate is that of seeking connection where, typically, you would not connect. At first, entertaining this additional level of connection might seem time consuming; however, in practice, it takes mere seconds and can foster unique problem solving abilities.

The Mirror Exercise

This is another exercise to broaden your gut awareness and combines physical and metaphysical levels; I originally learned this in an improvisation-based theater class in college. For years it marinated in the back of my mind before I included it in workshops. My workshops are creative-based healing experiences, and I love to see clients and participants from all walks of life respond to the ripple effects of this often foreign-seeming process. You'll actually experience three exercises combined. In addition, with a partner, you can practice your repertoire of moving through space in relationship to others. This exercise will help expand your experiences the next time you circle back to the exercises in Chapter 3.

I see great value in working with these theater games as a life experiment in shared space. In theater or any live performer/audience relationship, when we are dialed into our surroundings, we move beyond a functional relationship. In effect, we are living our dreams in shared space. Taking this metaphor one step further, if you connect your life purpose in relation to your dreams, we can say we are living in the theater of the world, living our dream-lives in the shared space of this planet, once again having the opportunity to grow as Inner Alchemists.

Three Types of Relationships

Through theater games, we can learn and identify three basic styles of relating. These are: symmetrical, complementary, and functional. Of course, I have adapted the classical games for our healing purposes, so if you're a theater major, you might see attributions to a complementary style and think differently from those without such a background. Remember, these three styles can be combined in myriad ways, but they serve as the basics to scan for yourself in any situation. Sometimes the type of relationship is obvious, but with any unclear or messy connections, understanding the three basic styles of relating will help.

An ability to track relationship styles can help you lower your alarm system. You'll be able to jump to decoding the "relationship game" and thereby short circuit a habitual trigger. This can apply both to your work relationships as well as your love life.

You'll also feel what your gut responds to and which scenarios hold strong energy for you. In this way, you'll discover what your primary relating style is. You can even check in with yourself as you did for the Grocery Store exercise. Is the attraction you feel to blueberries purely functional? ("I'm going to eat them because I know they're full of antioxidants.") Can you take your inquiry to another level as I did with rutabagas? Aim to surprise yourself.

Mirror relationships are symmetrical relationships. Select a partner and stand facing each other, arm's length apart. Decide who will lead and who will follow. The leader is the person looking in the mirror. That person starts a slow-motion, simple movement—arms only or legs and arms, whatever feels right. The follower acts as the mirror, attempting to do the same movements as those the leader is making, at the same time, in slow motion.

The leader's objective is not to fake out or surprise the follower. Rather, it is to be aware and take the follower along; if the follower falls behind, the leader might even hold her position until the follower catches up. When you become adept at the mirror exercise, both players lose track of who is leading and who is following. A true blending and melding occurs, and this is actually Craniosacral in nature as it's an exercise that helps foster empathy.

An observer of a truly blended pair would be hard pressed to identify who was leading and who was following. Think of the role mirror neurons in the brain are said to play in empathy. (We'll touch on that connection again after we've covered all three of the basic relationship styles.)

Make sure as you are playing this game that you take both the leader position as well as the follower spot. Try to vary your motions so that if you play one round washing your face with small movements, you lead using larger motions the next time, involving more of your body. Notice which size movements you're more comfortable with. You might want to relate that back to see how it informs your Energy Signature.

A symmetrical relationship develops from mirroring. One example of this relationship style is what the Neuro Linguistic Program people practice when they see you tuck your hair behind your ear and they follow suit. Another example would be teenagers wearing the same outfit, matching bracelets, similar hair styles, and even carrying similar purses. A good friend of mine landed a big television writing gig by mirroring her interviewer.

Complementary relationships involve true response. Complementary has nothing to do with compliments; rather it means complementary relationships need each other to exist in relationship. In traditional theater games, players work within the complementary construct in one of three ways:

1. Positive/Negative—an example would be a bully/the bullied.
2. Positive/Positive—classic mother/child (of course, if you didn't have a positive relationship with your mother, simply fill in a positive substitute here).

3. Negative/Negative—the best example of which would be complainers who feed off each other. (We'll look at a variation of this in Chapter 6 when we speak about triangulation as it relates to body-based therapy.)

So, you can see how it would be easy to find yourself in a complementary relationship and "playing your part" almost by rote, without conscious awareness. As an Inner Alchemist, encourage yourself to make these relationships conscious to the degree you can thereby transform unhealthy relationships. In the inquiry process, you can sometimes connect your role in a given relationship to a past, core relationship or core need gone unmet.

Let me deconstruct an unpopular example. Let's take the role of bully. From my observation, bullies are extreme examples of people who have needs unmet. They need that true response of the complementary type to feel superficially alright in their skin. They seek out an energetic "match" to complement their bully status, someone who will "allow" him- or herself to be bullied and complete the complement.

Please understand, I'm not equating "allowing" with gangs of bullies traumatizing a gay youth. But I do believe that if kids learned at a young age about their Energy Signatures and frequency matches, perhaps through these alchemical versions of theater games, they would have tools that might more easily stave off the bully's radar. Active bullies would experience options to achieve the "alright" feeling they crave, opening alternative behavior possibilities, which might eventually include losing the triggered compulsion to bully.

In my work, I've modified the classic complementary definition, de-emphasizing the negative/negative option, although it comes alive in the Triangulation-type relationship we'll discuss further in Chapter 6. In everyday life, you'll more easily notice this "feeding" type of negativity and make the choice to extract yourself from those kinds of exchanges.

Add in to this mix a concept of improvisation not part of theater games, the construct of "Yes, and...." This means if the person with whom you're in a relationship within any given moment brings something new into the conversation, you will include it, rather than negate it. Negating kills the possibilities to create, so our complementary relationships purposely build on each other.

Here's a positive/positive start:

"Say, Joe, thanks for cluing me in to the value of smelling fruit."

"Yes, and the tangerines smell wonderful."

"Yes siree, you look like you've been testing fruit this way all your life."

Now, if Joe chooses to say, "Oh no, I don't," he has negated. What happens then? The build ends, the game falls flat. Think of all the times you have negated in a conversation. It happens all day, every day if left unrealized.

For the purposes of these 30 days and beyond, you'll think of complementary as blending and employing a "Yes, and..." rather than a separation and denial of what's offered, as in "Yes, but...." This doesn't mean you pretend to like everything that's offered; rather, you simply won't deny or negate it. Instead, you'll consciously intend to integrate all offers if at all possible.

A wonderful example of this is an interview I held on my Internet radio show. I interviewed a Craniosacral mentor of mine, Eric Moya, CST-D, MFCC, about a course on resiliency he offers at the famed Esalen Institute in Big Sur, California. Although Eric has not, to my knowledge, been an improv performer, in fact, being interviewed is improv in a real world application. The interviewer/interviewee relationship is functional by definition, but solely functional interviews (with both people entering the conversation with the attitude: "This is my job, period") are forgettable or, at best, stilted. The best interviews are functional and complementary, like a jazz riff or a duet. I admit I asked a few long-winded questions in this interview. To Eric's credit, in true blending fashion, he kept his antenna up, looking for where he could connect next.

Ultimately, the interview was an example of a complementary relationship, filled with the intention of "Yes, and...." Eric self-identifies as a "systems guy," so soon after I uttered the word "systems," he was able to easily say, "Yes, and I'm so glad you brought up systems..." thus bringing key information into the interview flow. The result is an easy exchange, both of us in the moment and actively looking for places to blend conversation with information. Complementary relationship equals true response plus builds formed by "Yes, and...."

Let's transfer this games concept to a conversation with your doctor. That the relationship is functional sets certain groundwork. Here I'll recount a purely functional version as we eavesdrop on a conversation involving a dislike of a recommended course of treatment. I often hear clients recount this type of exchange.

Doctor: "This is my prescription for you. Take these pills every day twice a day."

Patient: "For how long will I need to do that?"

Doctor: "Based on current studies on patients with your condition, you'll be taking them for the rest of your life."

Patient: "No, I don't want to do that."

Doctor: "If you don't listen to me, I can't help you."

That's a fairly common exchange, dry and functional. Neither party has gotten what he or she wanted in that scenario. Rather, the doctor has a non-compliant patient, and the patient has an unwanted course of treatment.

The remedy would be to add in "Yes, and...." Be on the lookout for ways to create a complementary relationship within the functional doctor/patient relationship. Sometimes you may simply need to find a different doctor who'll listen to your concerns; but within functional relationships, sometimes a small win is what's possible. Let's face it, if you consult with a surgeon, chances are high he or she will suggest surgical options. Arguing merits of surgery in such a situation is a waste of your precious energy.

I'm not suggesting that all professionals are worthy of "Yes, and..." but you are worthy. Employ "Yes, and..." where reasonable and actively look for those opportunities to choose that option over "Yes, but...."

In both my many and varied personal experiences with doctors as well as myriad stories I've heard from clients, time and again I see that when the patient's approach changes, everything can change.

Here's a successful, complementary doctor/patient exchange:

Patient: "Yes, and I see that these pills are needed now. I'd like to come back in three months as you suggest. Would it be possible to discuss at that time how my body has handled the prescription and review my options? It's difficult to hear that at age 45 I'll have to take pills for the rest of my life. I'm sure you understand."

Doctor: "Yes. I can't say that there will be any new developments in research by our next visit, but let's see how your body tolerates the medication."

Hopeful, yes? The door is left open for the possibility of further discussion. You, the patient, have been heard.

We've already spoken about the third basic style of relationship in our improv game of life. Functional relationships include cop/guy caught speeding, professor/student, and store clerk/customer. Though these can escalate into emotionally charged relationships, you can often lower your internal alarm system by the simple act of reminding yourself that the basis of the interaction is functional. In these cases, one or both of you is doing a job. Essentially, it's nothing personal. If you find that your functional relationships often result in personal confrontation, then that is a signal to you that there's inner alchemy work to be done.

Here's a situation in which I thought I was entering a functional relationship and wound up utterly wrong. In the 1990s, right after my first abdominal surgery, I volunteered at a youth center called the Heart of Los Angeles (H.O.L.A.). I thought I'd be functioning as someone giving back to a community of youth underserved in the arts. Although my physical energy reserves were low, I instinctively felt the nudge to get beyond my pain and out into the benevolent world. My rationale was to assist existing children in case I couldn't have my own. One of the other volunteers, National Public Radio reporter Kitty Felde, started a one-act playwriting class with which I assisted. I figured it would be a clear cut teacher/student, functional relationship. As it has developed, over 20 years later, the class and the kids who allowed me into their lives are still informing me.

The secret to volunteering is that as you are helping others, they are, in fact, helping you. The wealth of experiences Liliana, Chainsaw, Henry, Mercedes, Haymen, Frank, Jose, and dozens of more amazing kids shared with me was embarrassingly rich, far more valuable, in my eyes than the tips I shared with them. The one-act plays produced at H.O.L.A. during the three years I volunteered comprised some of the best and most inspiring theater I've ever seen. I believe that's due in part to the constructs we used in the writing classes and the improv work being based in truth and nature.

I recall one exercise in which the kids were asked to pick two complementary forces of nature and then imagine a conversation between them. One boy wrote about a rushing river wearing down a magnificent large rock. This qualifies as a complementary relationship. Rivers need rocks. Rocks shape rivers. When asked about the "characters" and the story he'd envisioned, he said he was the rushing river and his mother was the rock he was wearing down. It was a poetic apology, a cry for help, and an unforgettably healing one-act play when his mother came to the show.

None of these kids went on to lives in the theater but, with the exception of Frank who died very young, they are now teachers, world travelers (Henry lives in Finland), and seekers of balance in a world where they were not statistically given good odds. The arts exposed them to perception-widening options and ways of accessing their unique gifts. The relationship with H.O.L.A., its visionary founder Mitchel Moore, and all the kids who I was lucky to know, elevated what, on paper, appeared functional but which combined all three relationship styles and resulted in a true moment in time forever imprinted on the chambers of my heart. As a ripple effect, the life-altering relationship to the H.O.L.A. organization also changed my relationship to the world as well as the worldview of those special kids. So my advice is to stay open and keep playing with the possibilities presented to you. You never know, you may get saved when you thought you were the one doing the saving.

Initially, one of the three types of relating will feel most comfortable and resonant for you. You can also use this as a tool to decode not only what type of relationship you find yourself in, but to check in with your gut as to what might be needed to alter a standoff or a misunderstanding. You might ask yourself, "Would mirroring this situation buy me time to figure out the best course of action? Is highlighting the functional aspect of this relationship the solution to resolve differences?" The applications are myriad once you are comfortable with the tool.

Now it's your turn to root out and detail your relationships.

Relationship Style Through the Years Exercise

Make a list of key relationships you can remember: childhood experiences, your siblings, teachers, coaches, first job, first love. Also, be sure to include more recent relationships and exchanges. Is there a vital relationship you have with an organization? Detail that using your senses and the heightened awareness you're developing, now that we're midway through our 30-day journey. After you've made that list, next to each entry write the dominant style of relating that defines the relationship.

You can and will have hybrid relationship answers, but be sure to list which style comes first. Which style did you lead with in your younger years as opposed to now? Ask yourself if that operating principle resonates with your gut knowing. Or has it been layered on by social conditioning, perhaps, thus masking your authentic preference?

This is a perfect time to revisit your notes from last week's You in Relationship to the World Exercise from Chapter 3. Using what you've now learned about the three styles of relating, go back over your notes and see what category you'd place yourself in—positive/positive? Or are you and the world complaining together? Collect the data. (Also, check in with You in Relationship to Others/Place.)

Mirror-Rebound-Space Rebound Exercise

Stand facing your partner, arm's length apart. Determine who will start.

Begin with the mirror exercise. This time, after you've switched leads and mirrored for a while, the follower will signal a switch to rebound by calling out, "Rebound-Complementary." The leader will make a gesture or movement in real time with an accompanying sound or a short phrase. Remember, you won't be able to mirror if you're jumping ahead, planning what your first rebound move and sound will be. Stay in the moment. Trust your gut.

The partner will rebound by making a complementary movement, not a mirror, and include an accompanying sound or short complementary phrase beginning with "Yes, and...." The response will build on that and continue on in a "Yes, and..." relay back and forth in real time until someone breaks momentum or runs out of steam. You may both even dissolve into laughter.

At that point, one of the partners will call out, "Rebound-Functional." It doesn't matter which partner. If you like you can decide beforehand, but after a time or two you'll realize not knowing is a fun challenge and more in line with how life happens, suddenly and sometimes out of thin air.

Now the quality of your movement will change. A sound or short phrase will become crucial at first to transmit who's "in charge." When both players start out as authority figures, this can be quite funny. To make the functional scene work, someone will have to give. See how this process works for you. Make sure you experience both roles. Notice if you're more comfortable as the authority figure or in the supporting role.

Try out at least three functional relationships. Notice any connections to your relationship style-of-choice in everyday life.

The final part of this game exploration is space rebound. This is a silent, slow motion back and forth between partners. Only one person moves at a time. In this game, you're playing with exaggerated, full body, sometimes animalistic movements. The chief rule is this: Your every movement must arise fully informed by and in response to your partner's previous move. No touching each other during the game. This is similar to playing chess with your body.

If you practice the games—Mirror, Rebound with Complementary and Functional roles, and Space Rebound—each for four to five minutes at a time throughout this month, you'll see how your everyday relationships take on a wider palette of possibilities. You'll find yourself coming up with new solutions to old issues. There will be a new energetic aliveness to even the common act of ordering at a restaurant.

Let's circle back to possible ways the mirror exercise can be self healing.

First of all, you must be utterly present to successfully mirror. When humming along smoothly in this exercise, your focus shuttles back and forth between what your body is doing, how well it's mirroring, and your partner.

It's not a huge leap from this deep, specific, careful awareness to include the experience of empathy. Looking in a mirror is usually done in private. It's a vulnerable act to make it public. Consciously being a mirror for someone is also a huge responsibility. For example, if your partner lifts her hand up to her eyes you may catch yourself thinking, "Oh. I know! She's going to rub her eyes!" Stay with that train of thought and you'll miss what your partner may actually be illustrating and sharing. Tune in, use your new tools, and sense her luminous field. Perhaps she's brushing away a tear. Don't ever assume. Mirror. And in doing so, you'll be inviting empathy into the relationship.

So, for a moment let's connect the mirror theater game you've just learned to mirror neurons. Mirror neurons were first studied in research with monkeys, seeking to determine whether or not they can help phantom limb pain. There's dissention in scientific circles as to the results, but for the scope and purpose of this book, to help you to foster connection and self healing on three levels, what is most appealing and apt is the connection between empathy and the role of mirror neurons. Mirror neurons are thought to explain the human ability to imitate motions, as we do in our mirror game. Mirror neurons have also been credited with helping us to understand the intentions of others. That is a key job description for people who work as actors, professional speakers, artists, and for any creative person. You are—we all are—people who create. Thus, these games from decades ago dovetail with our exploration of the potential role of mirror neurons today.

In phenomenology, empathy is defined as describing the experience of something from the other's viewpoint, without confusion between self and other. Empathy has also been described as identification with an understanding of another's situation, feelings, and motives.

When we become aware of another person's action, a number of neurons fire in much the way they do when we ourselves initiate an action or feel an emotion. In this way, the observer and the observed merge. Think, for example, of what happens to you as you watch an inspiring live performance or an inspiring performance in life. You connect, you merge. Those mirror neurons fire.

According to Newscientist.com: "Mirror neurons activate when an action is observed, and also when it is performed. Research reveals that there are mirror neurons that fire when sounds are heard. In other words, if you hear the noise of someone eating an apple, some of the same neurons fire as when you eat the apple yourself."[1] Again, according to Newscientist.com, in empathy tests, subjects who scored higher also showed higher levels of mirror neuron activation.

Wouldn't it be life-enhancing to be able to shuttle between empathy and objectivity on an as-needed basis? If you practice the tools you've been shown, with an emphasis on the games in this chapter, this is precisely what will happen for you.

The following story illustrates empathy and objectivity within an uncommon operating theater. Stress producing, yes, but you'll note some of the tools you've learned being put into action. You may never have a scalpel or a "sharp" in your hands as I did, but you can practice metaphoric connection via this story. Notice what stays with you.

Essay: The Anatomy of Connection

Several years ago, in Oregon, I met three cadavers. Actually, one cadaver and two heads. When I signed up for an unembalmed dissection class through the Upledger Institute, the class was six months away, too distant to seem real. Then all of a sudden I'm on an aerial tram run by the Medical Center gliding up a hill toward the Office of Body Donations.

During this four-day class, I know I'll need a Touchstone. I will need a daily dose of Bringing Down Heaven, as well as a frequent check-in with the You in Relationship to Place inquiry. My relationship to hospitals is one of sheer terror. Death and dying don't upset me. I envision death as a shrugging off of an overcoat no longer needed. I did hospice for my dad and watched him take his last rattling breath. But getting close up to a dead stranger's viscera seems rude. And "sharps," as medical folk call cutting tools, scare me. Still, if I can find my way into this, my work will deepen. The key, as in any Inner Alchemist work, is to allow the flow.

I step off the tram. The Medical Center buildings soar. Stage dressing aside, hospitals are not good places to spend much time alive. My motto has been "get in and get out fast." Now I'm here for four days.

When I find the office in the basement, I know there is a joke in there somewhere, but the irony wafts past. I meet the Director of Body Donations who looks like Santa Claus wearing a lab coat. Santa introduces me to Dr. Erikson, the dissection teacher who looks like a benevolent earth mother.

We 10 students gather to discuss protocol, expectations, and questions before we move into the dissection room, don our protective gear, and meet the cadavers.

We move to the dissection area to suit up. We are silent as we help each other tie the backs of the blue paper gowns and adjust plastic face shields. I learn to pinch the thin zinc piece at the top of the shield around my nose to keep the clear plastic over my eyes from fogging when I breathe. I place my grounding Touchstone in my pocket. We tuck our pant legs into paper booties. I wonder if this gesture is meant to protect me from death grabbing my ankles.

I overhear one of the teaching assistants saying to another, "Oh yes, double layer the gloves, I think we'll need that." I wonder what she knows. I double layer my gloves.

On the door, I read a cheery sign: "Here is where the dead rejoice to come to the aid of the living." I imagine *Twilight Zone's* Rod Serling speaking the line. No smell yet. Then I cross the threshold and take in more than I had planned. Our main body is lying supine; to her left sit two metal tables with indentations for the blood run off. Each table has a metal pan with a head placed inside.

Okay, I am officially daunted, except for one thing. I adore our full cadaver.

Our teacher says she died just shy of 100. I thought she would be lying face down because the primary focus in Craniosacral dissection is to observe the interconnectedness between the occiput at the top of the spine and the sacrum at the bottom of the spine. I wasn't prepared to see her face, open mouth forming a small "o." Oh, indeed.

Humans are full of juicy fluids, and our various densities are what make each of us unique. For me, seeing how each muscle flows into the next, how stress placed on one organ immediately impinges on another, is gorgeous proof of how everything is connected. The liver hears each percussive beat the heart makes and is impacted by it. In anatomy books, The Liver is chapters away from The Heart. In the body, they hear each other intimately.

We call our cadaver Charlotte. She is somehow prim, even lying face up, melting from her time in the freezer. In our old clothes, our scrubs, plastic face goggles, and double gloves we gather round. I don't know where to look first. I focus on her wispy hair. Then I slide my eyes to her feet. Her toenails, curved and tusk-like, remind me of my mother's. It takes me most of the first morning to allow myself to fully take in her face. I do, however, right away sense that the energy that was once Charlotte is utterly present in the room.

I chide myself that a more scientific therapist wouldn't be imagining a cadaver communing with us. I cannot waste this precious experience, afforded to so few, with flights of the senses. I focus on the already exposed yellow and pink abdominal omentum, which looks like an apron and acts like nature's poultice when a nearby organ is distressed. It can wrap itself around like a fluffy blanket and can aid in healing. It's also the part of us that is siphoned out during tummy tucks. I understand: We can either have a healing blanket that will tuck around a sick organ or we can fit into smaller jeans and let our organs fend for themselves.

As we look from the body to our Netter's Anatomy plates, each of us remarks on the way the anatomy books show body parts in different colors; I could use those codes now. The muscles and attachments don't start and stop, they flow into each other with no clear delineation—no vivid color changes like those in the text. So there's the liver, but where's the bright blue marking it as separate from the gallbladder? In this place the muscle is called one thing, but inches away it's called something else, though the flow is continuous. That is affirming.

The two heads are different stories. I can actually feel anger coming off one of the heads. Who knew that anger could be so corrosive it stays inside the tissues even after death? No one is drawn to work on either half of Angry Head. Over the four days, each of my fellow students tells me at one time or another that they sense either anger or outrage when they examine her. When it's my turn, I imagine her interior dialog. "What do you mean I'm dead? Where is the rest of my body? What is Craniosacral Therapy? How dare they leave me in this stainless steel pan all day?" What an unexpected way to utilize the You in Relationship to Others exercise.

The second head is resigned. His nose curves to the left, which might be the result of melting. If he could speak, I imagine a Brooklyn accent or a Jimmy Cagney crack. His is the hemi cut head, so I cannot see his eyes fully, and this adds to the gangster image.

After lunch, we work on the thorax, complex and layered. Our teacher has given us permission to address areas about which we are curious, those that directly relate to clients we have back home. One of my younger classmates dives right in; her exuberant hacking leads me to think of *Sweeney Todd* as she dissects an entire knee and ankle while we labor on the narrow avenue of the thorax. We are following the hyoid bone attachments, trying both to identify them and keep them intact. I attribute Sweeney Todd's zeal to her youth. I can't imagine someone closer in age to one of the cadavers, someone who had been in hospitals, near to being on this particular kind of table, blithely diving in with a sharp.

I want to hold a heart in my cupped hands, then a liver, then a spleen. I want to feel the difference in the weight, in the energy between the organs.

After a while, I take a break on my own. Outside the room, I remove my double gloves and see my hands have lost at least a pound. Through the huge windows I see the tops of gorgeous northwest trees. The first day flies by.

On our second day, the electric saw comes out. I'm not going near it. One of the physical therapists volunteers. We have to turn Charlotte over while maintaining the integrity of her body as much as possible after being filleted. I am uneasy; I move to one of the heads to probe the corpus callosum, which, like all body parts do, looks like a shape from the natural world, in this case like a shell. This calms me. I scoop out the cerebellum. It looks like a sea sponge washed ashore, albeit a metal shore. I spend the morning with my gangster head, as far as possible from the sound of the saw.

That afternoon we stand around Charlotte, having just seen the saw cut through to reveal the dural tube encasing the spinal cord. The dural tube looks like a pickled pink and deflated celery stalk, the cerebrospinal fluid no longer flowing. As one of the physical therapists and Dr. Erikson work to release some ribs for better viewing, I decide I will become a vegan. As I'm thinking this, it becomes necessary for someone in more or less my position exactly, to cut the tube to expose the cord. I refuse to lose my view, so I pick up the scissors and cut the fragile looking dural tube from the spinal cord. It's a small moment, nowhere near as boisterous and fleshy as Ms. Todd's deeds, but I know that for the rest of my life I will have that layered image to help me in my work.

I am on my break and marveling at the vastness of the forest outside when I become aware of someone in the corner by the stainless sink. It's Ms. Sweeney Todd. Her back is to me, she's bent over the sink, and I can see her shaking. I stay put. She turns around and sees me looking at her. She washes her hands and looks for a way to dry her tears.

"Just hit you?" I ask with a small smile.

She seems stunned. "Wow, you read my mind."

I say nothing, secretly glad she has caught up to herself.

On the third day, we experience our most startling observation and tactile experience. Charlotte is again on her back. Window cuts in the brain and removal of brain matter have left a gorgeous falx and view of attachments and stress marks. The stress lines look like hatch marks similar to those someone might daily mark off on a calendar.

Someone now has the opportunity to lightly place hands inside the window cuts, onto the falx; someone else will place a finger inside the mouth, up onto the upper palate, and touch the tiny vomer bone. I am the vomer bone person, and when I touch, the palate moves. The vomer bone shifts, releases.

The therapist on the falx yelps in surprise. Our eyes lock. Wordlessly we switch places. I place my hands through the window cuts and onto the falx on either side. It feels like rubbery butterfly wings. The other therapist begins the mouth work. The falx moves up then back.

This is a dead body and I'm getting releases similar to those I facilitate in living bodies. I ask our teacher about this, and she smiles and says, "Yes, isn't that something?" She leaves it at that. Some of my classmates rush to explain, others stand back in wonder.

On our fourth and final day, we assemble in the classroom. I'm exhausted. Someone takes a group photo. People ask questions. Sweeney Todd is reflective. I am full of awe. I also can't wait to throw out the clothes I've worn for four days straight.

It is customary for students to thank the donated bodies. Even in dissection class, ceremony has an important place. In the classroom, our teacher reads a poem about nature that refers to both a higher power and gratitude.

We suit up and enter the dissection room for the last time. The heart has already been exposed, but we pass it around and examine the attachments. It looks like deep water coral tubes. The posterior body wall shimmers. I am enraptured, and the morning flickers past, leaving behind a set of snapshots in my mind: the coral, the stainless steel, the blood run off from the sharps over the sink.

Then we must say goodbye to Charlotte. I want to cover her with her skin, the way you might drape a coat over your grandmother's back or pull a sheet up under her chin.

It's time for the closing circle. We hold hands and circle the three metal tables. Dr. Erikson starts to sing, a folksy, happy trails tune. With all our voices together the sound is haunting because some of us don't know it and there are stops and starts, like a round. We give thanks for this rare experience, for being right here right now. Part of me wants to leave for home and a Martini, but another part of me wants never to let go of the hands I am holding in this circle. I've glimpsed a micro universe, sacred spaces inside Charlotte with which my sacred spaces have resonated.

Finally, slowly, we peel away from the room, and in silence we remove our gear, walk to the classroom, gather our belongings, and find the elevators up to the sunlit paths that will take us on our individual journeys home. On the tram ride down I see fascia in tree bark. The river bank is a shimmering artery wall.

Recap of Chapter 5

Concepts

- ✿ The enteric brain, your gut brain.
- ✿ The three basic styles of relationships.
- ✿ "Yes, and..."
- ✿ Mirror neurons and empathy.

Tools

- ✿ A sensory connection to food via Grocery Trip.
- ✿ A sensory connection via the Orange Exercise.
- ✿ Your relationship styles.
- ✿ Mirror game—walk in another's shoes.
- ✿ Rebound—experience the three styles and true response.
- ✿ Space rebound—strengthen your awareness of the powerful "space between."

Chapter 6

Tracking Neutral—Is No Attachment to Outcome Possible?

The highest form of human intelligence is to observe yourself without judgment.

—Krishnamurti

The present moment is the only one available to us and it is the door to all moments.

—Thich Nhat Hanh

In this chapter we'll be working with the concept of Intention as well as Neutral. If your intention in any situation is neutral, in terms of unnecessary pain, confusion, and stress, you're ahead of the curve on all three levels.

Understanding the concept of Neutral can be a game changer for all aspects of your life.

Intention

Intention is defined as a course of action that one intends to follow, or an aim that guides action—an objective. As an Inner Alchemist, I see ripe opportunity for metaphorical application. So, of particular interest to me is the fact that another meaning of intention is found in surgical medicine, defined by the Merriam-Webster dictionary as: "The process by which or the manner in which a wound heals...the three degrees (first, second and third intention) are distinguished by the relative amounts and types of granulation that occur."

In discussing this with Dr. Patricia Ebert, D.C., she offered an analogy as to how physical wounds heal best. Dr. Ebert is the co-founder of Biodynamic Resonance Technique, a unique healing approach that utilizes kinesiology and energetically programmed vials to access the body's inner wisdom and remind the healer within of its innate potential. So it's not surprising that her viewpoint is expansive and metaphorically inclusive. She shared the following:

> *Like a newborn baby, granulation tissue is filled with potential. If the tissue is able to move through its normal range of motion, the healing process will align the new tissues in a supportive pattern, allowing it to tap its full potential. However, if the area is immobilized, such as by a rigid cast, the new tissue will heal with the fibers aligned in a haphazard pattern, similar to a pile of pick-up sticks. It will heal with a scar, its potential will be limited, and energy will be bound up in it.*
>
> *To free up this bound potential, the introduction of a new energy, will cause the fibers to re-align. Kind of like rolling your fingers over the pile of pick-up sticks will cause the sticks to re-align perpendicular to the direction you are rolling.*

What do you imagine the granulation might represent in an "old story"? Might resistance to healing hide in our "pick-up sticks" mix? Could granulation signal cellular confusion as to the manner in which to heal? What is the relationship between metaphorical granulation and a metaphorical rigid cast? Remember, the inquiry is meant to expand perception. Is there granulation potential somewhere in your body right now that needs re-alignment? Ask your body, questioning on all three levels. Go slowly and see what, if anything, bubbles forward for you. As you likely know by now, I'm intrigued by metaphor and in this case by the notion of releasing metaphorical bindings. Be sure to make notes so you can review what surfaces.

Neutral

The dictionary definition of Neutral doesn't take into consideration the levels and nuances of our application of the concept. A state of readiness is not impassive or indifferent. Imagine, for instance, an athlete—say a baseball leftfielder. He never knows when the ball might come to his glove. If he works himself into a state of tense panic, wondering when the ball might fly his way, he'll have sapped his energy and will have little left when the ball heads toward him. An overeager drive to catch everything, even centerfield-bound balls, will wear him to a nub. Does this image metaphorically apply to your life? You may occasionally need to assist your centerfielder, but if you can be in a Neutral state of readiness, you will avoid collisions.

Even in the unlikely event that you were to skip the exercises in this chapter, just grasping the concept will make you aware of Neutral as an option. Neutral is a magical state of awareness that we often whizz past as we rush from daily drama to daily drama.

When my clients practice tracking Neutral in their daily lives, they truly reap the benefits of the practice of shifting perception and remaining energetically available to respond to situations. At the same time, they're able to see choices.

Neutral isn't static. In other words, you can't acquire a Neutral state once and be done with the work. Rather, Neutral requires a shuttling of awareness that ultimately will become a practice. Just as your breathing pattern may be fluid now, in this moment, you know your breath can change in an instant—if you panic, your breath might become shallow and gulping, but when you are calm, it will be deep and full and still deeper as your breath sinks and elongates during meditation or a healing session. In a similar manner, Neutral rides ongoing waves of awareness that can change from moment to moment.

In life there is constantly incoming information. To maintain Neutral in the face of emotional or physical triggers, you must learn to check in frequently with your body. One way to think of this process is to remember the process of learning to drive. Likely, at first, you felt there were too many elements to think about, too many places to look—where do you put your feet? What about those mirrors? Other drivers? Turn signals? After a while, you learned to automatically move your gaze from the rearview mirror to the side mirror and then to look ahead. You learned to automatically shift your foot from gas pedal to brake. In much the same manner, as you check in with your body and learn to trust this process, it will become more and more automatic.

Think back to a personal story from years ago that shocked you. You'll know you've landed on a good example if, well after you heard or experienced the story, it still held a charge for you; if every time you told that story, your pulse quickened or your palms sweated or you felt like crying or you brimmed with anger all over again. Then one day, after some good talk therapy or after your friends rolled their eyes one too many times when you launched into the tale, you decided you would never bring it up again. That, you decided, would fix the situation.

But as you've learned in reading this book, old stories can lie dormant in your body, and their ability to trigger responses that you'd rather not own may well still be operating.

Neutral is not the same as burying or ignoring or understanding cognitively that a story has passed, the danger is gone, and the shock is no more. That is denial, and denial can be a comforting way station; however, it's not a destination. Cognitive understanding is valuable, but if you've been approaching an issue or a stuck place exclusively from the neck up, your physical body and energetic field will be out of balance and you'll overlook innovative solutions, unavailable to you because you can experience them only on a different frequency. In order to live in our authentic present, we want to capture those unseen solutions, see the broader choices. To do this we need to drop into our sensory selves, with a welcome mat out for Neutral.

It's also key to recognize that Neutral isn't a numb or stone-faced stance. You can't be mentally checked out and surfing Neutral. Neutral is, rather, a ready state with no attachment to outcome.

Body-based therapists disagree as to whether or not true Neutral is realistically possible. As an example: If you're working in the healing arts, your intention is to help, and by its very nature wanting to help is already an attachment to outcome. In other words, you're approaching a client with helpful rather than Neutral energy.

Still, honoring Inner Wisdom is a way into Neutral. My personal take on this discussion, metaphorically, is to shoot for the moon (perfect Neutral) and live among the stars (forget about absolutes and stay fluid). In other words, set the clear, grounded intention that you will reach inside and find what degree of Neutral is available to you in the moment. By doing so, you become more open to any outcome.

As you become sensitive to more of the signals that your physical body and luminous body send you while you are creating your daily practice, as urgencies arise within, or as you feel that a certain something *must* be done immediately, you'll know you're not in Neutral. You'll have a chance to reset by using any number or combination of the exercises you've learned: Bringing Down Heaven, Transformation Circle, taking a Touchstone Walk, and asking your gut what type of relationship is currently operating. You now have a window of choice.

A Matter of Urgency

In some situations, of course, urgency might be what's needed, but if that urgent feeling is accompanied by panic or a strong emotion, you might want to pull out one of your new tools. Perhaps you'll want to blow frustration into a stone or do three rounds of Bringing Down Heaven. You might want to work with filling out your Cinemascope peripheral sides or put yourself in Stillpoint, which you'll learn how to do in this chapter. Many clients come to me with a physical symptom enmeshed with what they have determined to be absolutes, and this often serves to compound their distress.

For instance, I think of many women who have come to me longing to get pregnant. They'll speak of being tired of buying baby shower presents for their peers and of being fearful that there is "Something wrong with me." Some who have endured long periods of taking fertility drugs and enduring expensive procedures come holding so tightly onto absolutes in the form of fear ("I must get pregnant and it has to happen during this round of drugs" or "I'll try alternative therapy for six weeks only, if it hasn't worked by then, it's not going to"), they leave little room for creating miracles. They cannot see beyond the necessity of conceiving within their time frame.

I must say before I'm accused of being harsh: I have been there. Years ago, my doctor gave me a you-have-a-small-window-here-last-ditch-effort talk. My self-assessment was severe, with no Neutral in sight. At the time, I assumed that if I were unable to conceive, I had no value as a woman. My luminous energy field was muddy, fogged up with others' expectations. Not only was my body decidedly not my friend, we had a war going on in my abdomen.

When I first realized I wouldn't get pregnant, I felt as if someone had died. Though the dream of having a baby did die, I chose, albeit with limited energetic resources and awareness, to live under the direction of the sage saying, "There's no going around, only through." I accepted what existed—no small feat. And it was only with acceptance of my physical limitations that I was able to move on to another layer and to create the life I was meant to embody.

I love babies and have great rapport with them in sessions, but these days I'm also glad to hand them back to their parents. What did I do to heal and find my reason for being? No surprise, it's what I'm offering now in a self-help version of Cranial Alchemy. The concept of Neutral enhanced my life, and it can enhance yours. This applies across the board in all the modalities I've synthesized for my system, not only Craniosacral Therapy, but also the theater games, the enteric explorations, and learning from a direct, focused relationship with the natural world.

A note about conceiving: Everyone has heard stories about a couple giving up hope of having a baby naturally, adopting a child, and then getting pregnant. This situation applies perfectly to Neutral. It also applies to my shoot-for-the-moon belief of what's possible with Neutral. If you can create in your central nervous system the state of a readiness without a "this better work" layer of anxious expectation, then and only then can something new have an opportunity to enter your experience. Whether the new is a baby growing in your womb or a different perfect baby solution, something will shift. Grace will make some kind of appearance. I have seen this happen time and again. The shift often centers on a surrender of perceived control. It centers on trust. And if you don't first unearth trust for your body, you will have difficulty trusting a larger force.

Having no attachment to the desire to have a baby may feel impossible or like a lie, but I've seen the process of coming back to that embodiment of trust result in positive outcomes.

As everything is connected, if you are reading this and thinking that conceiving and having a baby was never an issue for you or never a desire, guess what? You can simply replace "baby" with whatever you truly desire to create and conceive, and this advice applies equally. Neutral will shift naturally. Don't try to control it.

Because much of the human race looks around and sees control through force as the only way to be safe, finding Neutral and staying there is tricky. Bringing Neutral into your life and nurturing it in a sensory way on a regular basis is an act of bravery.

The Efficacy of Neutral

We all have blind spots. Fun fact: there is a spot in the retina of the eye where we literally have a physical blind spot. That said, in this chapter I'm referring to those situations or circumstances or events when we are certain we can't be Neutral. These are our blind spots, situations when we might even say, "How could anybody be Neutral in the face of...?" My personal examples would be horse slaughter or child trafficking. Surely, we think, there is no Neutral in those circumstances.

But the question to ask is what will effect change? How can one person make a difference? I'll concede that well-placed outrage and urgency can work in limited application. But through time, the toll is exacted on the outraged one. I believe true change comes via Neutral. I advocate we start a Mass Neutral movement and see how long it takes for positive change to take root and blossom.

Exercise for Finding Neutral

Checking in with your body, asking "Where is Neutral now?" is a good Touchstone question throughout your day. Then place your hand lightly on the spot. This simple yet profound tool can allow you to experience your "necessary" attachments anew.

The Craniosacral Direction of Ease Exercise

Lie down on a yoga mat if possible, or anywhere, but without a pillow.

Keeping your head flat on the surface, slowly turn your head to the right as far as you can easily go without forcing it. Don't lift your head up and then place it on the side—the move is a gentle roll. Now roll your head back to center and note how far you went and whether you felt stuck at a certain point or if the turn was completely fluid until your cheek was flat against the surface you are lying on.

Now repeat that move to the other side and come back to center.

Which side was easier for you? We'll call the easier side the Direction of Ease and the other side the Direction of Barrier. Because this exercise demonstrates what's possible using the Direction of Ease, turn your head back to whichever was the easier side and hold it there for between one and two minutes. Practice easily noticing what's going on in your neck, if anything, and allow yourself to take in the rest of your sensory awareness. For example: Are your toes curling? How's your breathing?

After a minute or two, turn your head back to center, and then roll it to the other side.

You should be happily aware that you can now turn further than you did at first. Whatever restriction was on the barrier side now is gone. I've seen this happen thousands of times.

You may be wondering at this point what just occurred.

After all, we weren't working on the Barrier side; we were focused on the Ease side. Well, you've now experienced, first hand, the power of the Direction of Ease as it applies to your body.

That was a physical level, self-help demonstration of the Direction of Ease, first introduced to you metaphorically in the story in Chapter 4 about the horse packing trip. You'll recall, the river rose, plans had to change, and we went in the Direction of Ease, following nature's dictates. In this instance, we can say we went in the direction the body was comfortable moving, as Dr. Upledger's teachings explain; we honored the resistance so the resistance had no force to come up against; it dropped its guard, so to speak, thus allowing access.

Cumulative Work

Remember the tube of light that you imagined encasing your spine in the Inner Reconnaissance exercise from Chapter 1? By now, you should be working a short version of that into your week as well as working with your Rebound tool and your Transformation Circle. Add in your Nature Hunt in the City and your Manmade Hunt in Nature as needed too! Have you been able to incorporate Bringing Down Heaven into your days?

Cumulatively, these exercises help to sensitize you. I suggest you feel comfortable with those tools prior to trying these next exercises.

Stillpoint on Yourself/Stillpoint on Others

A Stillpoint is a natural reboot of the nervous system. Stillpoint by definition is performed by a therapist on a client/patient, but you can put yourself in Stillpoint with a foam Stillpoint inducer.

For true do-it-yourselfers: Take two tennis balls, place them in a sock, tie the end of the sock in a knot to stabilize the tennis balls and keep them touching each other. An athletic sock works well. The bumps created by the balls are placed corresponding to the prominent bumps at the base of your skull. Lie down with this inducer, either homemade or store bought, and you'll be giving your nervous system a refreshing reboot. No more than three to five minutes is necessary.

You can also try putting yourself in Stillpoint in a seated position. You can do this anywhere and no one will know. It may have an added benefit of releasing back pain.

Sit comfortably in a chair with your back straight. (For this exploration, we'll be working with Inner Reconnaissance, Part One.)

Imagine your flexible tube of light and connect with it. Be aware of it encasing your spine easily. Detail it for yourself, using your senses, as if you had to turn a report in to someone who had never experienced or seen a tube of light such as this one. Is it clear or is there a color?

Now pick a spot on your spine. The first spot that comes into your awareness is usually best. If you have an area of recurring back pain, then by all means choose that. We'll call that the Restriction Point.

Imagine a beam of light coming into your tube and filling from tailbone (sacrum) just up to that Restriction Point you've chosen on the spine. With your Intention, hold that beam still until you truly sense it easily.

Once you're comfortable with sensing that, allow the beam to fill from Restriction Point up to the base of your skull (occiput). Then follow it back down to the Restriction, then down to your tailbone.

Follow the beam as it leaves your body. See it metaphorically beaming deep into the center of the earth.

Was there any change to the Restriction Point? Notice any changes.

Do this again in the following way: Now, this time, bring the light into your tube at the tailbone, up to the Restriction Point and hold. Then allow the light to flow up to the base of your skull again, only this time we're going to play with allowing *the restriction* to move as you image up and down the spine. This should feel different, with a loosening sense.

What do you notice?

Often, after trying this exercise both ways—with the light beam moving first around the Restriction Point, then with the Restriction moving with the light—the Restriction releases. Your Craniosacral rhythm drops into Stillpoint. A deep sense of calm infuses your awareness. You have put yourself into Stillpoint!

Stillpoint on a Partner

You can induce this mechanically until you begin to develop the sensory feel of the light rotation of the rhythm.

Sit in chairs facing each other if possible.

1. One person will place her hands on the thighs of her partner. Think of your hands as each being a leaf and the thighs as being water. Remember the energy exercises and what you learned about your Energy Signature in Chapter 3.

2. Now, with your light leaf-hands on your partner's thighs, see if you can use the sensory skills you've developed these past three weeks. Tune in to the waves beneath your hands, just under the partner's skin. If you imagine or "think" you feel a motion, go with it. Rotate your hands to follow that motion—it will be either an outward rotation or an inward one. This can be tricky to feel, which is why Stillpoint is being introduced only now, in Week Three. Still, it may take you longer to feel that rotation, but practice Neutral going into each try and soon enough the rotation will "jump" into your waiting hands.

3. Once you follow both the outward and inward rotation for a few cycles, the next step is: On the next inward rotation, manually and with intention stop and hold the rotation inward. Your hands will rotate inward, but not move from your partner or change position much.

4. Now you may feel no resistance, which means you've just put your partner in Stillpoint. Or you may feel an outward rhythmic push. If that's the case, stay where you are, hold fast but lightly until that resistance dissipates. The dissipation is the sign you've put your partner in Stillpoint. You can then remove your hands.

In both instances, you can manually "start-up" the rhythm after three to five minutes by lightly beginning outward rotation again. If you don't, your partner's rhythm will naturally resume in its own time.

Developing the knack of putting yourself or a partner, friend, or relative in Stillpoint is a skill worth taking the time to develop; you will find the benefits invaluable for stress and pain relief.

The Triangle

Another concept to work with at this point in your 30-day journey is a different type of relationship dynamic than those we've previously

worked with. Triangulated relationships are energetically birthed know-
ingly or unknowingly and can be harmful on all three levels. Talk therapists are qualified to attest to the psychological aspects. I work with the
adaptation of the concept called the Triangle of Disempowerment. I
re-learned this concept in a tactile, earthy way several years ago in my
Four Winds Inka Medicine Wheel work, but versions of it are found in
many spiritual and psychological teachings.

There are three points to a triangle and three corresponding roles.
These roles are: The Victim, The Perpetrator, and The Rescuer. Because
I anchor my work through the body, the inquiry in looking at triangulated relationships becomes, "Where is this role alive in my physical
body?"

In our lives we probably play or have an opportunity to play all three
roles at one juncture or another. However, unlike the three basic relationship types, Victim, Perpetrator, and Rescuer should be obvious in
this instance. Here, the objective in becoming aware of this construct is
to be able both to identify when we are unwittingly cast in one of these
three roles and to *step away from the triangle.*

This means we choose none of the triangulating roles. This is not
necessarily an easy task, especially if we've grown up identifying with
any one (or more) of these strong roles. Furthermore, if we received attention as a child by inhabiting one of these roles, we may not even be
aware of the triangles we unconsciously seek out or create as adults.

Take, for example, the role of The Rescuer. The person who self-
identifies with this role will exhaust his or her personal resources for
anyone perceived as needing them. The Rescuer will attempt to rescue
those people who don't want to be rescued with the same fervor they
rescue those who willingly enter into a complementary relationship. If
this behavior resonates with you, allow the concept of the triangle into
your awareness, and the next time you feel a Rescue tug, make a con-
certed effort to practice Neutral. Notice what tightens in your body. If
you are able to, ask yourself when was the first time that you remember
experiencing that tightening. Wait and see if your body expresses a com-
ment on that memory.

Some people consciously, even strategically, choose the triangle to deflect their own inner pain or disconnection. Psychology tells us that people who feel helpless may seek to relieve frustration through complaining. Remember back in Chapter 5, reading about the complementary negative/negative relationship possibility? In this relationship construct, the two need each other to exist. Having a secret with a third party can offer temporary, much-needed yet potentially harmful connection.

Because our work is body-based, it's vital that we look at the way family stories and ingrained conditioning can surface and how we can work with them through the senses, through our three levels of connective tissue.

As we delve into ancestor work, let's look at how it can influence your body and may run your energetic "show." Ancestral influences can be positive or negative or, in some cases (as described in the following essay, "The Healing Sword"), they may be both.

Even the most shameful ancestral events and stories can be transformed so that they no longer hold sway over you. As you've learned, it's all in how you hold perception. The solution to transforming challenging ancestral stories and events is not in simply pasting a smiley face on the experience. Yet often, families have a way of doing just that.

Elements of our ancestors, those we know of and those we don't, play a role in our Energy Signature. They are always available to you energetically. This can be welcome or scary news, or something in between.

For a positive ancestor as an example, suppose your grandmother has passed, and you need strength that you associate with her. You might summon "Grandmother energy." Two ways to connect with that energy are:

1. Intention that energy during a nature walk. Perhaps name it, "This is my Honoring Grandmother Walk." This is a method widely employed, for example, in charitable walks/runs. For instance, people walk/run for a cure to cancer, and the Intention is often the fuel. A great way to see how this works for you is to try two separate walks with intention for two different ancestors. Notice the differences that come to light. Some connections will be more powerful than

others. You may well have wildly different responses at different stages of life to the same ancestors. We're working with doorways to what's unseen but very real, energetically.

2. A second powerful option could be to make a Transformation Circle as you do your morning practice and choose "grandmotherly items" or include elements that your grandmother would have loved. Additionally, you might ask, as we do in Chapter 1's Inner Reconnaissance meditation, "Where is 'Grandmother' energy in my body now? Where is it influencing me internally?" And once you've located it, start the Transformation Circle or go on your honoring, exploratory walk.

One of my Medicine Wheel teachers, Lynn Berryhill, suggests creating a special area dedicated to honoring your ancestors "so you always know where they are!" Everyone chuckles when she says this, and if you're now smiling, I don't need to give you a less-than-positive ancestor example.

Even if you try the ancestor inquiry only in service of viewing choice, it's good mulching to question what's been passed down to you as truth through generations. Owning your own truth, not your family story, releasing cellular old stories that you may disagree with, that you didn't write, will make the ancestral view clearer. That will serve you, rather than you serving the ancestral story.

In the following essay, notice how I repurpose a shame story into a healing event. It happened because I tracked Neutral and was open to serendipity. When you are offered something new and different, outside conventional norms, what is your initial response? I used to be fearful or skeptical. Now I ground and practice self-referencing and, yes, set an Intention as to the reason I am trying the new experience. I then locate Neutral for the moment.

Essay: The Healing Sword

My father's great uncle George Khoutieff died when I was 8 years old. My chief memory of him was that of a thin, senile, bald man who could sometimes be found on our front porch waving an arm above his head, dressed in long johns and black slippers. My French-Canadian mother would scream "get back in here" and drag him inside, muttering to herself, "Old man thinks he's giving a speech to the troops."

I grew up hearing that he was a hero. The few Russian relatives and honorary relatives around Manhattan when I was growing up offered the utmost respect to Great Uncle George. That he lived with us was seen as a great honor to everyone except my mom, who bore the brunt of caring for him.

From South Ossetia, he was the last army general of the last Czar of Russia. All I knew about Russian history was the story of Anastasia and the mystery of whether or not she was still alive. Oh, I'd also seen *Dr. Zhivago*. My dad looked a bit like Omar Sharif, and when I was a little girl Russia seemed dramatic to me.

I had never heard of the pogroms. As a small child, I did pick up on a secretive quality, a presiding sorrow around those older Russians. This was palpable to me as an intuitive child. But even today, I'd like to think they were aware that the mass murder they either participated in or silently watched and accepted was shameful at best. But I'll never know. I do know that Great Uncle George was a leader. He pulled his family up from poverty into the larger world via his military career. Did he believe in what he ordered his troops to do, or was it just his job?

What's of interest to my healing journey is to unearth the strands of shame I cellularly associate with this ancestor. What might I have unknowingly soaked up of Great Uncle George that currently informs my well-being? This is the type of question you might want to ask of yourself as you entertain ancestor work.

I chose to work through what I own as family shame on my father's side. I am able to check in with my luminous energy field for threads linking me back to that time many years before my birth, and release what I find. Then, if indicated, work to transform yet another layer of connection lodged in my being. Often, when we think we've completed a healing journey, we've merely entered another layer of the healing spiral.

We lived in a three-bedroom house in Rosedale, New York. The downstairs bedroom was where George, or as he was nicknamed, Daddy

Goga, lived for the last five years of his life. I largely ignored him, but I do remember the last day of his life. The doctor came, said he didn't have long. My father wanted to dress him in formal Sunday clothes or at least a nice suit jacket. As he struggled to get Daddy Goga's arm in the sleeve of his black Sunday jacket, my father felt something heavy inside. He felt around and realized some papers were sewn into the jacket lining. He pulled Daddy Goga's arm out of the jacket; my mom got scissors. There inside the jacket was a bank book for 25,000 dollars, quite a sum at the time. My father panicked. Here the man was dying and no one knew about this money. He ran out of the house, jumped in his car, and drove off. An hour later, he came back with bank papers to be signed by George Khoutieff. By God, my father held his uncle's hand and got the signatures he needed. Then Daddy Goga died, and I started going to private school.

Soon after his death I forgot about Daddy Goga.

I was in high school before I learned about the pogroms. I should set the stage by saying that my answers to questions in high school came from a bit out in left field. Teachers liked me, I was studious and bright but, for example, when we were asked what constitutional body the United States was, I did research. I looked up my choices and confidently said out loud, "It's a republic." The teacher's face fell. He stared at me as if perhaps I was being a smart aleck. Then he simply said, "Jeannine, we're a democracy." I said, "What about the Declaration...and to the republic for which it stands...?" I wasn't convinced his answer was right! It's not a huge leap from there to understand how I wound up drawn to alternative healing.

At any rate, this was the same classroom where we learned about the pogroms, only this time I didn't open my mouth or raise my hand during the lecture. Shame spread through my neck, traveling slowly down my spine, black as thick molasses as I reconciled this history lesson with the family hero.

I inherited his sword—ivory handle, silver-tipped leather sheath. The sword was nothing ornate; it was a Cossack sword. I was the last

Khoutieff, so Daddy Goga wanted me to have it. I wasn't interested, so my mom put it away in a closet. There it remained throughout most of my life, including the decade I was married to a Russian Jewish man.

After my mother died, I revisited the sword, taking it out of the depths of a deep closet and placing it on a shelf, moving it closer to my life. But I wondered what shame, or worse, was attached to it. What arrogance was etched on that ivory hilt, that metal blade?

More significantly, what positive gift might there be for me to receive from the sword? I could not fathom a positive gift. I decided to bring ceremony into my healing process with this sword. I decided to metaphorically release any shame or arrogance from it. To thank the sword for doing what swords do.

In meditating with the sword and what it might hold energetically, I incorporated several Transformation Circles over several weeks. I connected sensory words up to the sword, slicing, cutting through, stabbing, slaughtering, waving, threatening, and finally a connection surfaced involving the modern day scalpels that had sliced into my flesh during two surgeries—doing what they were crafted to do. I made a list of all the family bonds I'd cut through and repurposed through the years. I did Touchstone Walks focusing on both ruthlessness and grace—represented by my father and mother—and discovered how in my life journey I ultimately chose grace, but surprisingly owed a debt to ruthlessness. Realizing viscerally that I owed George a different acknowledgement than my dismissal of his worth was the gift.

Two years passed before I finally learned about ancestor altars.

Ah, the perfect place for Daddy Goga. I'd be able to know where he was to ensure that he was not energetically informing my life any further.

Then Marianne Williamson spoke to my writing group.[1] "Place something on an altar and it is altered," she offered. That statement elegantly sums up a major benefit of creating ancestor altars.

But there was yet another ceremony waiting for me at an innermost swirl of my ancestor healing spiral. I didn't know what that was until one day I arrived at Sara Fancy's horse class to find that everyone else was a no-show for that afternoon. Because I don't believe in coincidence, the thought crossed my mind that there might be a special opportunity about to show itself.

We sat under a canopy of trees as Sara asked me what I'd like to work on. The herd was grazing close by, and Silver had an ear cocked listening to us. It came to me that perhaps I should try Sara's Healing with Horses. She works energetically with her herd of horses as witnesses, and I was attracted to the nature-based, equine-based session she offered.

This was a new, unknown experience that I was about to enter into. What allowed me to reap the most benefit from the unusual situation was the following:

- ❀ I set an Intention.
- ❀ I was clear about Neutral throughout the ceremony.
- ❀ I stayed with my body and tapped into its wisdom.

So though you may or may not be interested in trying such out-of-the-box experiences, we all are presented with opportunities to try new experiences, and by now you have specific tools to help you navigate whatever comes your way.

I ducked between the metal fence bars and entered the round pen with Silver and the herd. What unfolded in the present moment, with my awareness of the three levels plus Source, did not directly involve interaction with the herd. Horses have enormous energy fields, huge hearts, and I felt surrounded by what I can only call an invisible safety net. Remember the exercise from Chapter 3, You in Relationship to Place? This place provided a safety net for my exploration. Silver and the rest of the herd nearby held space while holding their distance. If I wanted to, I could now create a Touchstone for that invisible horsey safety net to call on and utilize in future unknown situations.

My intention for the session was to find ease in my body, to cease going about my own healing work by creating a crisis in my energetic field, to somehow prove I could overcome it before moving forward into my next purpose. That paradigm was not serving me.

I stood in the center of the riding ring facing Sara. I closed my eyes and practiced a space rebound with the environment. I moved my body from side to side while breathing from my belly, then waited for what felt different, which in this case was that the winds picked up. I then responded from there, rebounding with the wind, which allowed me to stop my mind's linear what-have-I-gotten-myself-into chatter. Being able to ground myself, but be open to the unseen and perhaps unexplainable, allowed me both to honor my process and to be open to Sara's.

By keeping my focus directed within my body, I soon became aware of a heaviness under my right shoulder, running down my armpit, and surrounding the right side of my luminous energy field. Sometimes, the act of focused noticing in and of itself allows trapped energy to release.

The heaviness did not go away. Sara asked me to describe the heaviness. I said without censoring my stream of consciousness, "It's ornate as though it's a good thing, to be honored but it's not mine." She continued to ask, and soon it became clear that the heaviness belonged to a holster. I've never actually worn a holster, but as a true Inner Alchemist, I allowed what surfaced from my Inner Wisdom to enter my process in classic, "Yes, and..." fashion.

"Is there anything in the holster?" Sara asked.

"I'm not certain. No, I don't know," came my answer. Inside I was reeling, wondering what this could possibly relate to. I knew that part of me did know. So I stayed with the sensations in my body and also the urges my arms had to move. I allowed them to move as though I were a marionette being moved by ancient strings.

In slow motion, I moved my left hand under my armpit and reported back, "It's a long pistol."

I felt compelled to energetically pull it out. The sensory flash I got was that it was silver. I followed my arm movement as it slid horizontally across my neck, which made no sense, but I had no attachment—I was being led by my arm, along for this sensory ride. The invisible pistol and my arm rose and stopped, and I saw I was now holding it close to my head. Hmmm. Physically, I stayed where I was, holding that position so I could feel into it, inventory my body.

Sara asked, "What it's for?"

"I'm feeling as if I'm supposed to wave it around, it's for show, there's some kind of circus feeling I'm getting." Then, after a few moments: "I'm supposed to do something with it, but it's not mine."

For a second, it crossed my mind that the position could be that of Victim. Was I meaning to shoot myself? But checking in with my gut gave the lie to that possibility. So I hung out there with my hand near my head waiting, without a clue, but open, Neutral, poised for information.

If you're not the Victim, then who are you? I wondered silently.

Suddenly it dawned on me. Aloud to Sara I said, "My father's paternal lineage were Perpetrators, they were highly decorated murderers."

"Military?" Sara asked.

"My great-great uncle George was the last General to the Czar." I spit out the next word, "Cossack."

I felt like throwing up. I alternated that with feeling faint. But immediately I felt lighter. I'd made a gut connection. The marionette feeling went away.

The entire experience lasted 30 minutes. The awareness of how the sword might become a healing sword was instantaneous. One fallacy about change and transformation is that it's a process. Setting the stage for transformation can be a step-by-step process, which is a benefit of this book, but the moment of transformation actually occurs in an instant.

Sara and I left the ring. We talked about ancestor work and how my life path of service was a path that might only have been possible because it arose from that which needed healing in my father's lineage. Another gift.

That the Cossacks lived with their horses, a thought I had only while I was driving home from the session, served to further my feeling that the universe conspires on our behalf to offer us scenarios in which we might heal, if we will only show up for ourselves. Opportunities await us if only we will notice. The space held by the huge heart fields of the herd allowed a safe container in which to explore. I could, in that arena, shake off a feeling of wearing a heavy cloak, my arms moved through space as though breaking down energetic cobwebs and toxins.

When I arrived home, I pulled the sword out of its drawer. I held it gently and eyed it afresh. It has since become a Touchstone to remind me that ruthlessness and grace were entwined in my DNA cauldron and that each of us has disparate elemental pulls. A blade can cut to hurt or cut to heal. Relief sometimes arrives in the unlikeliest containers. Via ceremony, Inner Wisdom, and horses, I have forged a healing sword.

Healing with Horses was a fascinating experience that I may well have missed out on had it been offered to me 10 years prior. Back then I might have worried about whether or not I was following instructions correctly, or I might have wondered what my linear friends would think and say. However, now that I have sensory-based tools that are so second nature to me, I allow myself to immerse myself in nature, honoring my ethics of staying with the body for answers and further inquiry.

You have now been working with, marinating and simmering with key tools in my system for three weeks. During our fourth week you'll work with sounds and specific situations to utilize all the tools you've learned.

Though you may never find yourself in a ring surrounded by a herd of horses and drawing an energetic pistol from under your arm, the next time you find yourself faced with the unknown, you'll have a way to stay with it if there seems to be alchemical gold in it for you; or, alternatively, you'll have tools to leave when your gut says this is shady. Most important, you'll know that it is authentically you shying away or embracing an event or a person and not just your conditioning, whether ancestral, cultural, or peer based, pushing and pulling you.

That is truly freedom from bindings.

Recap of Chapter 6

Concepts

❀ Working with Intention.

❀ Working with Neutral.

❀ Working with the unknown.

Tools

❀ In a stressful situation: Ask, "Where is Neutral now," with hand on belly.

❀ Identify the three roles in the Triangle.

❀ In which role have you been cast?

❀ Step away from the Triangle.

Week 4

Music, Sound, and Daily Life Remedies

Chapter 7

A-B-A-B and Sometimes C—Music and Sound

Spoken language was originally a swirling garment of vapor and breath worn by the encompassing earth.

—Ogotemmêli, an elder of the Dogon tribe of Mali[1]

Evidence is mounting that the universe expands and contracts like an accordion.

—Astrophysicist Harlow Shapley

No human culture has ever lived without music. Whether chanting mantras along with the gorgeously primal sounds of Tibetan monks, bopping to The Beatles, or shimmying to a pop song, the universe is forever breathing a musical breath.

In light of Harlow Shapley's quotation above, it seems the universe must be breathing a happy, goofy, musical breath—accordions are fun and silly, never sad. Whenever possible, I choose to linger in the sweet, goofy, musically breathing universe! In this chapter you'll have the opportunity to create Energy Infusions, utilizing an element of music structure. Once created and anchored in your body, you can call on Energy Infusions to quickly feel better in almost any stressful situation.

That music is healing is so deeply intertwined in some cultures, as reflected in the Chinese alphabet in which the character for medicine includes the character for music. The derivation of the word *music* itself is from the Greek *mousikê*, ultimately derived from *mousa*, the Greek

165

word for muse, and had to do with the arts under the dominion of the nine Muses. In India, the musical Vedas and Upanishads were specifically used for healing.

The concept of perceptual reciprocity, first coined by phenomenologist Maurice Merleau-Ponty, states that to listen to the forest is also to feel oneself listened to by the forest,[2] and that concept made deep sense to me when I recently experienced a healing of my luminous energetic body via a Peruvian shamanic drumming meditation. The powerful drumming put me into parasympathetic mode so that my body had the opportunity to begin its healing process. In essence, I felt heard by the drum. We'll play with this idea in the exercises in this chapter, substituting sounds and music for Merleau-Ponty's forest.

The benefits of music on health can include both physical and metaphysical stress reduction. People employing healing with music report results that include lowered blood pressure, pain relief, as well as experiencing a sunnier outlook on life. Sound frequencies composed solely by nature are also healing, as you can learn from the guttural, resonant work of pioneer Emilie Conrad. Or perhaps you have experienced feeling a sense of peace ripple through your body after listening to a recording of whale sounds.

On the website FractalEnlightenment.com, researchers note that the sounds of "birds, frogs, running water, etc. soothe the mind. All these natural harmonics vibrate at 432Hz and it's the natural frequency of the Universe."[3] Fractal Enlightenment goes on to say that even our DNA can be healed by the 432Hz frequency. This certainly is a prescription that would do no harm. Such ancient instruments as Egyptian wind instruments, Tibetan singing bowls, and Japanese *shamisen* have been discovered to be tuned to 432Hz.

The ear is the first sensory organ to begin working. In utero, the ear develops during the third through the sixth week of gestation. Babies are hearing noises and sounds as early as the eighth week in utero. We begin to listen before we see, smell, taste, or touch, so it is no wonder that our nervous systems respond in such deeply reverberant ways to the way everything sounds.

"Sound is linked to the physical body by the eighth and tenth cranial nerves. These carry sound impulses through the ear and skull to the brain. Motor and sensory impulses are then sent along the vagus nerve (which helps regulate breathing, speech and heart rate) to the throat, larynx, heart and diaphragm."[4] Vagus is Latin for *wandering,* and, boy, does this cranial nerve wander—from your skull to your gut. That sound is transmitted along this lengthy humming corridor helps to augment the physiological explanations of the releases that are routinely facilitated by working Craniosacrally along the vagus nerve.

Humans respond to both rhythm and resonance, and next we'll try an exercise with ancestor sounds that access both. To distinguish the two we can say that rhythm refers to external, toe-tapping mirroring wherein the heartbeat matches the source of the stimulus sound. Resonance comes into our awareness when we experience compatible frequencies. Some sound healers teach that each organ specifically corresponds to a different octave, and, indeed, in my work with sound frequency music, I've found that deeper tones mirror and resonate with the lower parts of the body. Gongs, which are often used in sound healing, resonate in harmony with the sun, moon, and planets and communicate a healing aspect of the Music of the Spheres. This notion was first written about by Pythagoras in the sixth century, B.C. Ceremonial associations with the sun, moon, stars, and planets can link us back to our natural state of connectedness with the world.

Recall your Touchstone Walks from Chapter 2? Try one focused on sound and music. As a result of a Touchstone Walk with this specific focus, you may discover a sonic Touchstone, an aural healing resonance that your body responds to, which may have been previously overlooked on prior walks.

Throughout time, man has imposed his will on the music of nature. I grew up hearing that in 1939 Germany, Joseph Goebbels, the Nazi minister of propaganda, imposed his will by changing the standard tuning pitch from 432Hz to 440 Hz. Centuries earlier, in 590, Pope Gregory the First is thought to have changed the mathematical relationship between notes, which had first been discovered hundreds of years earlier by Pythagoras. Asserting dominance over nature for no purpose other than dominance is ego based and ultimately limited in perceptual scope.

Nature always prevails. The natural tones patiently await our remembrance. The frequencies are humming along, just waiting to be met. Though our modern technological world drowns out or diminishes those natural tones, consciously seeking them out is a healing habit, one this chapter is designed to help you cultivate.

If, for example, Asian and Middle Eastern sounds and minor key wind chimes evoke a haunting somehow familiar resonance in your bones, these might be the sounds in your cellular memory of nature's music of the universe. For others it might be Celtic pipes or African drums.

Rests in music are another concept important to explore. In music, a rest is defined as a purposeful, rhythmic interval of silence. Metaphorically, a rest is the musical version of the physical Stillpoint you learned in Chapter 6.

Rests occur naturally in many languages. When I was a young girl, I heard both French and Russian spoken in my home. Sound figures strongly into my Russian ancestor awareness, like the clinking sound of ice in a highball glass. Russian rests are drama-infused, elongated pauses, before and after punctuation, like the pause before the firing of a bullet and then the moment of recoil. What comes into your awareness regarding rests in your ancestral language? What about your current pattern of speech?

Do you habitually pause before you speak or does a torrent of words tend to fly out of your mouth? Those are two ends of the spectrum of possibilities, of course, and you are likely to fall somewhere in between. By trying the following exercise inquiry, you may discover the way the language of your ancestors informs you today.

For example, my French sounds are lighter in frequency. For me, the rests in French contain a questioning quality. The sense I most associate with my French ancestors is auditory. However, more than rests, my French ancestor sounds are those of silence, of wind through tall grass, of a wooden roller shaping pie crust dough.

Exercise: Ancestor Sounds

1. Choose an ancestor you're familiar with. Or pick an ancestor you've heard a story about. Alternatively, if you've never heard ancestor stories, focus on that individual's language of origin.

2. What was the quality of that ancestor's first language? Was it soothing? Staccato? Guttural? Perhaps it's a language filled with rolled "r's" and melody? Write in your journal about the quality of your ancestor's sounds. Using your senses, as you've been doing all along in this book, the next step is:

3. Identify which senses are in play for you with regard to that language. This won't solely focus on hearing. Describe those senses, liberally employ adjectives, and soak yourself in those senses.

    Those language sounds reside inside your bones and if you invite them to, they will ripple forward. If English is the first language on both sides of your family, drill down into the accents, the syntax of the decade, the varying colloquialisms, and the unique music of your ancestor language. Allow it to inform you.

4. Jot down any awareness that surfaces. How do those language sounds make you feel? Where is that feeling in your body? Place a hand there, using the leaf-on-water Craniosacral touch you learned in Chapter 1. Metaphorically speaking, we're looking for musical connective tissue.

After my grandfather died, my paternal grandmother married a Columbian man. They traveled the world together but lived primarily in Spanish speaking countries. When I was growing up in New York City, I heard Spanish all around me, but when I visited Mexico City at the age of 10, I heard the phrase *en tonses* for the first time. In fact, I heard it so often I was certain the phrase had to be an important one. I learned it means "and so." As a result, I consider *en tonses* a musical rest.

In theater game terminology, it might also be viewed as a "Yes, and..." because it's suggestive of a build; the implication is an invitation to continue the conversation. My grandmother explained to me that *en tonses* is mostly used in formal Mexican Spanish, not in the colloquial Puerto Rican Spanish I most often heard in New York City. Although my ancestors were not Spanish, this is an example of a musical language phrase.

I invite you to seek those kinds of peculiarities as you delve into your ancestor sounds. Look for places where the language serves as a musical rest. Look into how ancestor language informs your central nervous system.

Another thread of connection exists between the three relationship styles discussed in Chapter 5 and the way sound frequencies merge. Using the concepts of wave interference, there can be either constructive interference or destructive interference. Certainly there are many wave variations, but for now let's define the basics.

Constructive interference occurs when two waves of identical frequency merge. When they do, they create a sound that is double the size and frequency. This can be viewed as a complementary relationship, in this case building to double the frequency.

Destructive interference occurs when two waves are combined and cancel each other out. This can be seen to be a version of a symmetrical relationship. Think back to a time when you might have dated someone "too much like you," or "great only on paper." Your sound waves may have cancelled each other out, thus contracting rather than expanding you as a couple.

Another negating example can be seen in Chapter 5 when Joe stopped a build in the produce aisle scenario with "No, I don't." With "No," we contract and diminish the collective, connective frequency. Imagine the expansive possibilities you might lose if you stayed within the confines of the mirror game, only serving as the originator of movement and never taking the exercise to the response level. If no build ever occurs via your action, the empathy that you might foster by mirroring never has an opportunity for further expression, expansion, and healing.

The spaciousness that accompanies sound can frighten some people and temporarily shut them down. A person who grew up associating sound with fear may well feel more comfortable with hushed tones. Don't assume you know what another person needs. Still, we can lay our collective tools at each other's feet and see where there is frequency match and where there is dissonance, then explore gently and bravely to ascertain whether the sonic imprint we currently express in the world is, in fact, in synchrony with that which we would like to express.

Then we can broaden our awareness so we either change our circumstances on a cellular level or enjoy hanging out with the higher frequencies. Itzhak Bentov in his book *Stalking the Wild Pendulum* delves more deeply into the notion of connectivity when he refers to higher frequencies as source. As he writes: "The broader our frequency response, *the larger the number of realities in which we can function.*"[5] Bentov takes the discussion to the highest absolute, which, as he says, in non-manifest form is pure potential, intelligent energy.

In college I took a music appreciation class taught by a frantic Slavic woman who loved that my last name was Khoutieff. Beyond that, however, neither of us had any idea what I was doing in that class. I had mistakenly thought it would offer me easy credits. However, during that class, I did learn two perspective-altering principles of music.

First, I learned the concept of sympathetic resonance and I translated it metaphorically to my everyday life as best as I could. Second, I learned the structure of written music, the A-B-A-B of it, followed by the occasional C.

In music, sympathetic resonance explains the reason that, if you walk into a room full of pianos and play a middle C on one, all the other un-played pianos in the room start vibrating to the frequency of middle C. I once tried this in New York City's Steinway store on West 57th Street across from Carnegie Hall. It was the weekend following the lecture on sympathetic resonance and I couldn't resist walking into the store with its floor-to-ceiling glass windows. All the piano covers were open—I figured this was so the strings might be viewed. After I hit the middle C on one, I looked closely and not only could I hear the vibration, I could see the middle C strings vibrating. It was a magical experience that anchored the concept of sympathetic resonance for me though this was decades before the book and film *The Secret*[6] made popular the concept of vibrational attraction.

What happens to create sympathetic resonance can be expressed technically in the following way: Itzhak Bentov writes, "Striking the middle C on a grand piano—the string vibrates at 264 Hz. Counting up the scale, the eighth string, an octave higher, will also be vibrating quite strongly in harmony with the middle C string. It vibrates at exactly double the rate of the first C, 528 Hz."[7] Other strings will vibrate as well but at less intensity, and the exchange of energy at fractional ratios is not as high.

This might explain why not all your friends are your best friends and why being in love frequently doubles your sense of your capabilities.

We access the internal harmonic beat that develops when the natural vibration frequency of one mechanism is in phase with a vibration of another mechanism. The connection from piano resonance to vibrationally humming humans is visceral. Regarding our vibrating bodies, Bentov continues: "...we can make a reasonable assumption for the existence of 'bodies' made up of the higher harmonics of our physical body." Luminous energy field, anyone?

Metaphorically, sympathetic resonance might also explain that pull you sometimes feel toward one stranger in a crowd. Getting in synchrony with the chords being played or notes being struck inside yourself can give you a wider and deeper understanding of all relationships.

So we circle around to the field of pure potential, rippling out and becoming you, becoming each of us in physical form, a motley crew of middle Cs on grand pianos worldwide waiting to experience sympathetic resonance.

When we think of music and sounds, we must also include the sounds that our body produces—both those we can hear, such as gurgling tummies and gulping breath, and those hidden elegant sounds like the bass track of the heart pumping and the whoosh of blood flowing through our arteries. I recall having an ultrasound and hearing sounds reminiscent of futuristic outer space film scores. When I said that, the technician laughed and told me he had had a few composers in his lab room who asked a lot of questions. I suspect they were inspired by those sounds. I personally appreciated the inner space/outer space connection.

Many cultures will break the fourth wall at the end of a performance, thus conceptualizing art. Oftentimes, in these sorts of performances, folk music or dance will be used to convey that all of us are, in fact, on a world stage, or as Shakespeare put it, "merely players." Specifically, think of classic Bollywood film endings where, no matter the ending of the film story, all the characters move into frame and begin to dance and swirl to music. The actress playing the lead might link arms with the actress who played her character as a little girl as they spin around. Even those characters who have died over the course of the film story will dance in synchrony with those who survived. This visually demonstrates the continuum we all are part of.

Take a look back at your notes after the exercises in Chapter 3, especially You in Relationship to the World, and see how music plays a role.

Think back to my story about Strider, the show I danced in on Broadway. *Strider: The Story of a Horse* has a sad ending. Strider dies alone, and audiences who attended our previews walked out of the theater in a somber mood. Just before opening night, the choreographer and music director devised a tarantella-style folkloric song and dance to add to the end of the show that transformed the perspective of the audience. This time, when the theater emptied, the audience's energy had shifted, and though they left the theater pensive (after all, it was Tolstoy), they were also invigorated. As a result, we enjoyed a year-long run of the show.

A-B-A-B is about composition. In my music appreciation class, I assimilated the idea that every once in a while in a piece of music after A-B-A-B-ing along, there will be a place to create a C, where a C is obviously needed. Maybe it's the bridge—and isn't that the perfect term? Once again as I learned this, I made the metaphorical leap to living a life. Generally, we go about our A-B-A-B days same, same, same, but all of a sudden a C will appear—that C might manifest as an important phone call, a moment of serendipity, picking the winning ticket, feeling a sudden clarity about something, discovering an inner knowing, or sharing a knee-knocking kiss.

Yes, we live in a musically breathing universe with bridges and unexpected Cs that appear in the midst of our routine A-B-A-B work. That those Cs resonate with each other through unplayed instruments flutters my heart.

Where in your journey through life have you found resonance thus far? Where do you hold that resonance in your body? I'm asking about the Cs. We've all experienced them. Throughout this book I've detailed ways to recognize awareness levels. This should help you be more aware of those levels of Cs.

For example, in Chapter 4 I told the story about collecting bird feathers for my project and noticing a small grey dove feather on my back patio. This was the kind of ordinary element that, through my Transformation Circle work, I had attuned myself to recognize on my newly recalibrated radar. For me, that grey dove feather was a C; it interrupted my A-B-A-B morning. Although its quality is different from falling in love with and marrying my best friend or from hearing transformation-breakthrough news from a client or, as you'll see in this chapter's essay, being remembered vividly by the boy who sat behind me in 6th grade, it is a C nonetheless.

By nature, Cs are alchemical, encompassing what might appear to be ordinary, but turn that A-B-A-B-ness into the extraordinary. Cs can heal. So you'll want to collect them.

Whenever possible, let's make them musical as well.

A C Exercise: Finding and Highlighting Your Cs for Easy Retrieval

Music, metaphor, and your life of Cs can anchor in your body and become either Touchstones or Energy Infusions (which is what Cs are really all about). This exercise is a start toward choosing what will become for you Energy Infusions that are on call anytime. Have your notebook ready.

Part 1: Settle in to walk down memory lane on a C treasure hunt.

Types of Cs

❀ The highlights of your life. For example:
  ❀ being first in your family to do a double back flip.
  ❀ being the first in your family to graduate college.

- ❈ the moment you landed a big account.
- ❈ the moment you created a charitable organization.
- ❈ meeting your soulmate.
- ❈ growing a sustainable vegetable garden co-op for your neighborhood.
- ❈ rescuing an animal from certain death.
- ❈ Small moments of bliss or zing, meaningless to anyone else but significant to you:
  - ❈ finding that grey dove feather.
  - ❈ the perfect parking space opening up just in the nick of time.
  - ❈ smiling at the moon in the night sky.
  - ❈ nabbing an elusive taxi in the rain.
  - ❈ swirling frosting on cupcakes with a child.
  - ❈ slipping a coin into the expired parking meter of a stranger.
  - ❈ finally connecting to a lesson a teacher taught you years ago.
  - ❈ washing your dog without getting soaking wet yourself.

As you write out your list, note that these Cs don't necessarily come into our awareness chronologically. That's fine. Capture them as the body/mind recalls them. You may wind up with quite a long list.

Choose half of your list in the following way: Go down the list and sensorily bring the event into your mind's eye. Notice where in your body that you sense a connection with the event. Place a hand there. Choose one word or short phrase to describe the bodily sensations. Note that word next to each C. You'll probably have overlap. So if, for example, four of seven Cs on your list have "Peaceful" as the evocative word, narrow them down to the one or two that give you a more immediate gut connection. In this way, you have Energy Infusion Cs of a peaceful feeling.

Fleshing these out with senses, as you have been practicing regularly now for the past three weeks, will give you a conscious sense memory to call on when you need an infusion of "peace" in your day or a counterpoint to a stressor or feeling of being on high alert. The key is detail and specificity within your body.

Part 2: Choose a C from your life and its attendant sensory components.

Write down all the components that you recall at the time the C occurred. Who was present and how (in sensory terms) would you describe those people? What colors were predominant? Drill down into what those colors felt like: Heavy? Smooth? Airy? What sounds were there? Timbre of voice? Weather-related sounds? Was there music?

After you've filled out all that you recall, try the cross-pollinating exercise by writing a second list of what that C brings up for you currently. Plant the "what if" seed—what would it be like to taste sound, smell sound, or see a C? Does the color "spring green" sound like a different instrument from the color "ice blue"? Play with mixing and matching. Not all your mixes will resonate, but if even one creates a ping, you may be onto a way to anchor that C in your body for easy retrieval.

We want these Cs to become Energy Infusions for you, available for you to call up in stressful circumstances. Remember the five-second rule you might have learned as a child? In that game, if food fell on the floor and you picked it up within five seconds, it hadn't "gone bad." For the purposes of this game, use the five-second rule to switch your focus from the stressor to the C swiftly and successfully, thus avoiding headaches and related pains.

Sympathetic resonance and the energetic field that precedes you into a room are part of the alchemical mix that creates Cs. Your energetic field is what people react to when they first meet you. Cs are in complementary relationship or mirroring relationship fields (remember rebound from Chapter 5), blending and melding. If your field is muddy, dissonance is fostered. If your energetic field is in tune with a higher vibrational frequency, get ready for an abundance of incoming Cs.

Play with the next exercise. Each of the systems in our body has a resonant set of frequencies in its field. I experience connection between body systems and musical instruments and groupings of instruments. I happen to relate percussion instruments to the digestive system, but if you get a sensory draw toward tubas or flutes in relation to your tummy, those will also work. The idea is to relate music to your body in a fun, visceral way so your internal listening skills become varied and deeply personal.

Let's explore that connection in the following exercise.

Orchestra Exercise: Your Body as an Orchestra

Begin with five minutes of Part Two of Inner Reconnaissance. At the end, imagine your body as an orchestra. As part of this inquiry, you may want to ask:

- ❀ How does your body operate differently as a musical body?
- ❀ Does one section of the orchestra primarily have the stage?
- ❀ What piece of music comes to mind when you imagine your body as an orchestra?
- ❀ Which of your senses aside from sound come into play?

When in synch, melody is created consisting of layered elements each doing their part, creating cohesion, balance, a crescendo when called for, and diminuendo when needed. Not every situation calls for an entire orchestra, though. We don't use all our available energy for every situation. Likewise, dinner for two celebrating a promotion might call for a cello or a three-piece combo, whereas winning Olympic gold might well call for a full orchestra or even incorporate a marching band.

To carry out the metaphor further, feeling suddenly elated might call for a clash of cymbals or a clarinet solo depending on your RAS and its set point. For another person, a clash of cymbals might be shocking and scary. This exploration is meant to be personal and non-linear.

As I mentioned, for me, percussion corresponds to the digestive system; thus my task becomes to break that down. That gurgling in your intestines? Intestinal communication. What might the intestines be communicating? "Great nourishment!" or "Uh oh, here comes trouble" or "Give me more!" Often, the sounds are physical releases. Look beyond and ask what *quality* of sound is being released.

For example, let's attribute the wind instruments to the lungs, the respiratory system. What quality of sensing does that bring forth for you? Perhaps the cello or a different string instrument resonates with the heart. Or would your heart sound more like a violin, viola, or harp? Entertain relationship in unlikely places, and foster it when you find it. Your world of possibilities will flourish in synchronistic ways.

Here's an example of how I incorporate a metaphoric orchestra in my own work. Say I'm working hands-on with a private client. Ultimately, this work is not about technique but about process. Sometimes I feel as if I am playing a part in a duet; sometimes a chamber music piece; and each time I feel I have never played this piece of music, but somehow the notes come to me just in time. The sound that rings out to me might be from the wisdom of a chamber of the client's heart or from a rumbling in the digestive system. Both releases, both awarenesses, but different frequencies and resonances. I would not say to a client, "Oh, your heart sounds like a harp." Rather, that would be a discovery for the body's owner to make, should he/she feel so called. The assignations to which I've given body parts and instruments is meant simply as a jumping off point, a template for you to use on both locating your Cs and in re-conceiving pain by elevating your perspective to the metaphorical.

The following essay recounts a relatively recent C, with at least a rock band's worth of resonance. This one spans 45 years. The part of my body it relates to is my throat, and the instrument is the kick drum. The color is navy blue. There's a feeling of summer lightness surrounding this C. There is a texture of smooth caramel present in my awareness of this Energy Infusion. I'm not certain what that might mean, but as in the Yellowstone Nez Perce story, I don't need to know. Rather, I need to re-conceive my senses, recalibrate them via regular inquiry. My job as Inner Alchemist is to notice and allow, to follow.

By now that should seem perfectly normal to you; if you've been doing the exercises in this book every day, you should be regularly having your own conversations with body parts and bringing your senses to bear on those conversations.

Whenever I need a swift kick into summer lightness, I flash on this Energy Infusion.

Essay: A Social Media C

In grade school I attended three private schools. Two of these were on Long Island, New York. My experience at Woodmere Academy, where I spent 2nd grade, was forgettable. I lasted only one year. The next two years were C years. I spent them enrolled at Sands Point Country Day school, adjacent to the ocean in a robber baron's converted summer home. It looked like Tara from *Gone with the Wind,* except in lieu of Southern majesty we were on a cliff on the North Shore of Long Island. My favorite school, by far. We had science class down by the beach. Our classes had just 12 to 15 children, so as we explored the grounds each day at recess, we felt expansive spaciousness. The grounds included a half-acre of tall, hedged maze we ran through, getting lost in the green spirals of *Alice in Wonderland*-like sculpted greenery.

My parents had recently inherited a decent sum, and although I made friends there, every other kid was rich, and I knew my family was not. This dissonance wasn't an issue held in my body—actually, that sweeping property allowed me a freedom to run without ever encountering a fence, and I dreamt dizzying dreams walking to class via curved marble staircases. It was a sensory Energy Infusion, a C, bar none.

Due to ballet classes I was taking in Manhattan, my parents moved me to a school in the city. I spent 5th through 8th grade at PCS, the Professional Children's School in Manhattan where lots of child models, actors, and sons and daughters of famous folk went. There were also lots of ballet dancers. I was shy, studious, the opposite of almost everyone else there.

In 6th grade, a musical family singing band called The Cowsills enrolled in our school. There were four of them, three boys and their little sister, each in different grades. John, the drummer, sat behind me that year in Miss Nitze's class. He was tall, had a Beatles haircut, and he smiled a lot. He spoke quietly, not like the other, more boisterous boys in our class.

After a month or so of school, The Cowsills were on the covers of all the teen magazines. Our class was small, and largely female, and we felt proprietary toward John. To the rest of the world, he was dreamy

John Cowsill, part of the famous family band that included their sing-ing mom. They had several hit records. But to us, that one year, he was just John, our classmate and our private teen idol.

The other boys were jealous. I recall that year we all switched from French lessons to Spanish class because of one boy's famous father. The father was so famous that when he wanted his son to learn Spanish so he could practice it during the summer visiting his movie set, an official school announcement was made suspending our normal French classes; suddenly we were saying *Si* instead of *Oui*. Well, it could have been co-incidence, but then I don't believe in coincidence.

Another boy classmate was co-starring on Broadway in *Oliver*, and the only other boy was a French transplant whose father was an artist who restored antique stained glass panels for cathedrals all over the world.

Alas, despite their credentials, none of the three other 6th grade boys could compete with John Cowsill for our affections.

Here's my 6th grade truth. I would have sworn John barely knew who I was. There were stunningly lovely girls in our class, girls like the model you met in the essay in Chapter 2, "Sparkle Hip." When the Cowsill family left before the end of the year, as suddenly as they'd arrived, I was devastated. John was gone forevermore, only to be glimpsed on television specials.

After 8th grade I attended the famed High School of Performing Arts. No more professional children. We were all happy amateurs, study-ing and finding artistic expression, working on (ahem) our instrument.

Through my teens and 20s, I heard news about John Cowsill via one classmate who relayed that John played drums for Jan and Dean. Later, I heard John lived in Ojai, which sounded romantic and richly creative. I imagined him up on a hill, musical, and "happy, happy, happy" as the Cowsills sing in their hit song "The Rain, the Park and Other Things." What a gorgeous, sweet boy to have known, albeit briefly.

Years passed, and I heard that John Cowsill was the drummer for The Beach Boys.

Then, one day, the summer I was 55 years old, a Facebook message flashed across my screen.

"Helloooo. Wait, do you remember me?"

I laughed out loud. I couldn't believe who was writing. I wrote back, "Are you kidding, John?"

Later, as we conversed online, after I'd confided my experience of 6th grade as brutal, he responded, "You were so beautiful. Like a Russian princess." Just like that, in an epic C of a moment, I was gifted a re-do for my invisible 6th grade self-image. Then he wrote, "I was so scared in that school."

We never would have guessed, John.

That new 6th-grade self-image is now available to me to call upon. A wound no longer, a part of myself re-cycled and handed to me with a thread of grace. It's anchored as a gorgeous ping of a C that alters my previously grooved ripple effect from 6th grade on outward. That's what Cs can do.

Since that first conversation, I've had dinner with John and his lovely wife Vicki Peterson (of The Bangles fame). I now know that the girls in 6th grade were right to feel protective of him, as at the height of his fame he endured emotional and physical abuse, abuse that has been since detailed in Louise Palanker's 2013 Showtime documentary, *Family Band: The Cowsills Story*.

At dinner, Vicki leaned in to me and said, "It's funny he has such strong memories of you and the girls in that school. He was there less than a year."

Although I understood why she might say that, I understood the connection differently. Dinner was neither the time nor the place to talk about childhood frequencies or old stories lodged in a body. Though I did want to tell her how it takes but a split second to reflexively be pulled back in time to a moment that strongly speaks to you, is alive inside you, even after decades have passed. But the restaurant was noisy, the meal was ending, and the circle was complete. Driving home, I got the feeling that raging hormones and fame aside, our nutty classroom must have been, in a weird way, the sanest place John knew at that heady moment in his life, our girlish smiles somehow a safe haven.

Soundscaping Exercise

As children we first enter into language by actively making sounds—by crying in pain and laughing in joy, by squealing and babbling and playfully mimicking the surrounding soundscape thus entering into the specific melodies of the local language, our resonant bodies slowly coming to echo the inflections. We thus learn our native language not mentally, but bodily.

—David Abram[8]

Practice this alone with the three words I'll give you. Later, you can try it as a guessing game with friends. Using sounds, you are going to try giving the words meaning by only the manner in which you say the word. You may repeat the word or part of the word; you may elongate a vowel or make attendant sounds to punctuate the word; but utilize no other words to get the meaning across.

Here are three practice words:

* Crash.
* Delicious.
* Gurgling.

There is no right or wrong way to try this. Let's break down a fourth word together: Cleansing.

Start with the first sound, "kl." If I play with where in my mouth I start the "K" and then add in the "lllll" and hold that "l," I'm reminded of the sound of a shower faucet—that sound you hear just prior to the water gushing out.

Next: the sound of "eh." Keeping with my first image of a shower, I may elongate that sound to convey positive aspects of this word.

Next: "N." I play with stretching out the sound "nnnnn"—where do I feel it? In my nose, up through my cheekbones. I play and notice.

And now onto "sing." My first urge with this part of the word is to break it up. My gut sense is that the "G" might need its own moment at the end, but I'll wait to put all my experimental sounds together in the word and see how it feels, how it sounds in the moment.

Here's another musical way someone might break down the word into only two parts. Clean-sing, as in pure singing of perhaps a single tenor or soprano. What does that deconstruction repurpose for you? Clean versus unclean? Clean as innocent? Clean-sing as a children's choir, or clean-sing as the chant of monks intoning sutras?

As you know by now, there is no right answer, only the answer that is right for you. This exploration is literally expanding the way you sensorily experience language. Play with the words and pause in between breaking down the words to see which sounds resonate in your bones, your organs, and your connective tissue. Seek to surprise yourself with the sounds that you create.

Secret Language Exercise

As a child, did you ever have a secret language with a friend? I did in 3rd grade with Carol Teitelbaum. It was a combination of French and whatever sounds we could make by puffing out our cheeks or curling our tongues, clicking our teeth together, and elongating vowels. We had a lot of fun and somehow managed to get our points across with our made-up sounds and larger-than-life gestures. Of course, we wound up laughing uncontrollably.

Maybe you had a stuffed animal or imaginary friend with whom you spoke in hushed tones.

In this exercise, I invite you to engage in a gibberish or fake foreign language conversation with a friend.

Choose a friend and a general topic for discussion.

Separately, write on a piece of paper (careful to keep your friend from seeing it) the point you want to make; one crucial point you want to convey regarding your topic.

Give yourselves three to five minutes.

After you have had this conversation, in your normal language discuss what you thought the other person was conveying to you.

In workshops, I hand out topics and participants draw from a hat the crucial point they must convey. This exercise works equally well when you and a friend decide on your own topic.

Open-Ended Exercise

Actively notice the sounds you make throughout your day. Seek out how those sounds can make music: Tapping a pencil, opening a bottle top, walking with a friend and falling in step—all these (and more) offer you potential sonic splendor.

Afterward, write in your journal a note about the music you made today. Be consistent with this exploration for this final week.

Recap of Chapter 7

Concepts

❈ Perceptual reciprocity.

❈ 432Hz.

❈ Musical rests.

❈ Sympathetic resonance.

❈ A-B-A-B and sometimes C.

Tools

❈ Working with ancestor sounds.

❈ Energy Infusions.

❈ Body as orchestra.

❈ Body as soundscape.

❈ The Music in Your Day.

Chapter 8

Remedies for Specific Situations

When my pain became the cause of my cure, my contempt changed into reverence and my doubt into certainty. I see that I have been the veil on my path. Now my body has become my heart, my heart has become my soul and my spirit, the eternal Spirit.

—Rumi

Furthermore, we have not even to risk the adventure alone; for the heroes of all time have gone before us, the labyrinth is fully known; we have only to follow the thread of the hero-path. And where we had thought to find an abomination, we shall find a god; where we had thought to slay another, we shall slay ourselves; where we had thought to travel outward, we shall come to the center of our own existence; where we had thought to be alone, we shall be with all the world.

—Joseph Campbell

Now is a good time for you to take out your stories from the Chapter 3 exercises and review what you wrote. Your sensory response to those stories may well have changed over the past 30 days. Using what you've learned during this entire sensory journey, check in with your body to see how your perception has altered. In the margins of your notebook, jot down the shifts. Soak in how brave you've been in choosing an examined, considered, gut-connected path to augment your health, creativity, relationships, and your life. If you've been consistent with the exercises, you now probably own a new, trustworthy clarity with regard to choices available to you.

Now that you are:

❀ practicing your Inner Reconnaissance meditation.

❀ finding a few Touchstones.

❀ on the lookout for signs of nature and embracing them daily.

❀ choosing the Direction of Ease whenever you can.

❀ working your Transformation Circle.

❀ playing with your Energy Signature out in the world.

❀ trusting your gut.

❀ consciously setting Intentions.

❀ practicing the tracking of Neutral.

❀ inviting musical rests into your daily communication.

❀ listening to your body as it reciprocally listens to you.

I invite you to retake the following Alchemy quiz. Immediately after you have retaken the quiz, note the answers that have changed from the first time you took it. Congratulate yourself on those shifts, both small and large.

Following this, notice those areas where you have stayed the same—areas where you feel stuck and those you identify as challenged. I offer specific remedies to address many areas where you might get stuck and triggered by people or events.

So first, the quiz:

1. What part of your body do you love without reservation?

2. How long did it just take you to answer Question One?

3. Which of the following best describes how that loved body part feels? A) Flowing like a waterfall, B) Glistening like sap on a tree, C) Smooth as a rock, D) Sparkling like a crystal, E) Other, please write it in.

4. Now, what body part frustrates you most?

5. How long did that question take to answer compared to Question One?

6. If you could have a conversation with that part to explain your frustration, what would the conversation sound like? Give a voice to that part and flesh it out with as much detail as possible. For

example: Does it have an accent? Does it have a lot to say or very little? Give yourself three to five minutes and see what comes up for you, if anything. Which of the following fit? A) A loud argument B) A tearful monologue C) It's lost in translation D) A gentle whispered "Hello, how's it going in there" conversation E) I can't do this

7. My daily level of stress is: A) High—off the charts B) Medium C) Low D) Stress? What stress?

8. If my spine was an animal, I imagine it would be: A) A quick, gliding fish B) A buzzing bee C) A fossilized turtle D) An octopus E) Other, please describe.

Quiz Question Updates

❀ Question 1: Ten points for being able to identify a body part you love without "buts." Were you a reader who answered "heart" on the first quiz go-round? Perhaps this time a different truth bubbled up? Give yourself the five points back if your answer truly is heart. I hope the inquiry processes in this book and the questioning of "heart" gave you an even deeper appreciation of your whole body and the messages it has for you. If you still aren't certain, try the following, short inner inquiry for clarity: Sit comfortably with both feet on the floor. Lightly place one hand over your heart. Say hello. Ask your heart if there is some other part of your body that needs attention right now. Now simply wait. Allow. Remember, just be open to what may bubble forth. Give this time. Begin with Part Three of Inner Reconnaissance from Chapter 1 if you need to center yourself for this exercise.

❀ Question 2: If you answered Question One right away, 10 points. Less than a minute, five points. Five minutes or you're still not coming up with a part you love, zero points. If you are still challenged by this question or even if you're happily surprised by a new awareness or sensory responses available to you: I invite you to inventory for yourself the body parts, both internal and external, that you find easy to relate to. Many people can identify the location of their pain, but now let's identify the specific strengths of each element. Where is there vibrant health? And, for example, what does vibrant health of your lungs look like, sound like, versus vibrant health of your skin? Go back over the sensory exercises with the information you've discovered about yourself via your new quiz answers.

❀ Question 3: If you were able to easily give a description, give your-self 40 points. If this was challenging, great; no points, but we'll work on that. Refer to the pages of descriptive, sensory words at the end of this chapter. Practice reading down the list and feeling how your body reacts to those words. You'll find some words will "click" into resonance with certain parts of your body. Remember, it takes roughly 30 days of practice to create a new habit. Stay with the list. As you become comfortable, you may want to add to the list. Ultimately, those added words will be the most powerful because they will have bubbled up from your Inner Wisdom.

❀ Question 4: Notice whether you jump to an internal part or an external part. Add five points either way. At this point in our ex-ploration, it's valuable to notice whether your tendency is to choose internal or external parts exclusively. We're after a balance for op-timum awareness, although with that said, there's no right and wrong here. Just notice.

❀ Question 5: Ten points for question five if it took you a long time to answer this (three to five minutes), zero if you answered right away, and five points if you had to think a minute. Were you slower responding to this question the second time around? What's your sense of that—not intellectually, but rather your felt sense?

❀ Question 6: 10 points if you didn't draw a blank. In the event that dialoguing is a challenge, why not play with the orchestra exercise in Chapter 7? Choose an instrument to "speak" for the body part. Choose the first instrument that pops up for you. Sometimes tak-ing away the need for words allows you a deeper experience or sense of relationship.

❀ Question 7: Pretty much everyone taking this quiz is A or B. Five points for either answer. Eight points for C. If you answered D, you get 10 points. For any lingering concerns on lowering stress levels, any of the myriad exercises presented in this book can lower stress. There will be a combination that will work for you. Mix and match to create the practice for you. I suggest you re-visit any exercise that you might have glossed over or avoided and include it for the next few weeks in your day.

   ❀ Question 8: 10 points for any answer and for gifting your spine with imagery. If the octopus choice appealed to you, wonderful; if not, I suggest you check online for videos of how the octopus moves. There is an economy of motion in undulation. There is a fluid sense of purpose to the movement as well as a luxurious quality. Wouldn't it be nourishing to find gems in the movements of nature's creatures and then find your adaptation of those qualities to incorporate into your own daily movement? Even if this fluidity were expressed by a few non-linear languid stretches before you get out of bed in the morning, consciously moving the way an octopus moves can be a great way to start your day.

In the following, you'll find suggestions for moving forward depending on whether your tally showed you to be a Fluid Alchemist, a Searcher, or an Inner Apprentice.

80 points or over—The Fluid Alchemist, Update

Your continued work will be to polish and refine, sometimes deconstruct and repurpose all the elements you have available to you. Deepening into a fluid relationship on all three levels requires rechecking in with your body dialog. During this process, you had the opportunity to ask myriad questions of yourself and put yourself in varying situations with Intention. Choose one or two questions from chapter exercises (not the quiz), and go forward with those seeking to anchor them with Touchstones for yourself.

Which questions leap out from memory right now? Choose those. "Where is Neutral now?" is a good one that will stand you in good stead across many a day.

40–80 points—The Searcher, Update

The tools you've acquired will deepen as you surrender and trust the messages your body sends you. If this notion still feels daunting, I suggest Inner Reconnaissance meditations to quiet the mind. Be sure to anchor the habit of asking the questions: "Where is joy now in my body? Where is fear? Where is humor?" Of course, on any given day, if you have an odd ache or are grappling with an emotion other than the three from the basic Inner Reconnaissance, fill in that blank in your questioning. "Where is _____ in my body?" and wait. Be sure to be patient and allow the authentic answer to bubble up from your sensory Inner Wisdom. I'd also suggest making sensory exercises, such as Walks with Intention in Chapter 3, a regular part of your week.

Under 40—The Inner Apprentice, Update

Still an Inner Apprentice, are you? Notice how that expresses itself in your body. See where in your body Neutral is around that notion. Let's build from that Neutral awareness. I suggest staying the course and re-reading the chapters that you might have glossed over. I'm always fascinated re-reading chapters of intriguing books and often find gems that were somehow hidden from me in prior readings. I find, too, that if I initially read a chapter while I am also processing a new set of tools, my retention of the material will be sketchy at best. Your success with this process involves doing, not just reading, but you've been absorbing a lot of material. A refreshing re-read may be just the ticket.

So, take a deep belly breath and if you haven't created a Transformation Circle for yourself as described in Chapter 4, that's a fun way to dive back into self inquiry. Honor your processing time just as you've learned to honor resistance. If you worked the exercises and read the essays, at some point along this journey some expansion and sense of spaciousness in your body should have been a welcome surprise to you. How is your attention span? Be honest as you ask yourself where in this book's process you checked out. Where did you perhaps lose interest? Oftentimes in discovering that place, you'll also discover a clue, and if you sit with the "I wonder why" of it, you can glean key tidbits as to who or what is "running your inner show."

I trust that your Inner Alchemist work will serve you well so you can create your life and health at the highest frequency possible.

Remedies for Specific Situations

Here are some examples—menus—of sample practices during your days and stressful situations paired with possible solutions. Of course, you may want to create your own solutions à la carte.

Morning Rituals

1. **Morning Ritual: Two Minutes.** As you get into the habit of this work over 30 days, you will find the time—you'll stretch time—to fit your alchemical, self-healing needs. However, there will always be last-minute, unforeseen dashes out of bed that leave your well-planned routine in the dust. So, with two available minutes here's what to do:

   ❀ *Octopus stretch for 30 seconds before you get out of bed.* Two nonlinear stretches. Make one a diagonal, reaching up from the fingertips of one hand and stretching down through the toes of the opposite foot. Then switch. For the second 15 seconds, try undulating, curving, and curling your spine as easily and gently as you can. You might wind up in a fetal position or a backward C curve—allow your body to lead.

   ❀ *Ground and Intention for 90 seconds.* As you rise, before you brush your teeth, wiggle your toes on the floor. Choose a grounding stone—I currently use a smooth, thin, black and white chrysanthemum stone—however, any stone you choose will work. Feel its weight and then focus on its lightness. Now hold the stone in your other hand. Notice any similarity or difference between hands. Bring into focus whatever is rushing you, stressing, or whatever you're dreading or is challenging you today and blow that into the stone using both hands to cup it. Now think of something you'd like to bring into your day, something joyful you intend to create, or something you are grateful for. Blow that into the stone. Once you have made this ritual your own, you'll see that this explanation took longer to read just now than this two-minute morning ritual will take to perform.

2. **Morning Ritual: Six Minutes.** Octopus stretch for a full minute. Lying flat, do the Direction of Ease exercise from Chapter 6, turning your head right, then center, then left. Sense which way moved more easily and turn your head that way, in the Direction of Ease. Hold it for 30 seconds then move back to center and then the other way. Feel the additional release. Total time: two minutes. Upon rising, begin Bringing Down Heaven, three reps, three leisurely minutes.

3. **Morning Ritual: 15 Minutes.** Follow the previous steps for ritual one and two for a total of eight minutes. Then spend seven minutes with your Transformation Circle. Try illustrating the way you feel early in the day, and refer back to the Circle later in the day. Another way to use your Transformation Circle is to Intention and illustrate physical areas you want to pay attention to and for which you want to show gratitude throughout your day.

Mid-day Breaks

These are, on average, 15 minutes each. Depending on your break location, one of these will work best. Feel free to put two together if you have extra time.

1. **Mid-day Break One.** Either a nature hunt in the city or a Touchstone Walk. Give yourself 10 minutes for the exploratory walk and five minutes to jot down a few notes about your experience.

2. **Mid-day Break Two.** Especially if you mostly sit during the day, try moving your spine in an undulating octopus-like motion while still seated. This is not a floppy or fast motion. Rather, imagine you're moving through a jello-type substance and make the move slow, languid, and easy. Stop if anything feels uncomfortable. Three minutes.

   As you rise from your desk, focus on your breath, imagining the tube of light from the Inner Reconnaissance meditation in Chapter 1. Five minutes.

   If you're stuck inside the house or office, take the remaining seven minutes to walk around listening for sounds in your environment, whether they are cadences of coworkers' voices or a slight drip from a faucet. Incorporate the hum of an air conditioner and the particular rings of cell phones. Be deliberate. It will be refreshing, especially if you don't tell anyone what you're doing.

3. **Mid-day Break Three.** Find a quiet place. Close the door, lie down. Practice sinking into a 15-minute Inner Reconnaissance, adding in "Where is _____ in my body," filling that blank in with anything that might have come up that morning; anything, that is, that you would like to let go of.

Your Commute Home

Walking. If you typically walk home, make a Touchstone Walk at least once a week. Practice looking for evidence that the universe is conspiring to assist you in both great and small ways. I walk the equivalent of half a block from my office to my home, yet even when I'm certain there's nothing new to see, if my antenna are up and I'm open, something new will appear. Perhaps it's a grey feather as in the story in Chapter 4, a sound of a dog I don't know walking by, or a group of fallen leaves that have landed in an interesting pattern. I actively look for a sign of nature's grace. I nearly always find it. Now if you so choose, you will also.

Driving. In some cities there are signs on apartment buildings near highways that say, "If you lived here, you'd be home now." Why not play with that idea on your next drive home? Take what you might know about an area you pass en route and imagine who lives there. Use your senses to fill in who you would have to be in order to live there. This works in your favor whether you choose a more affluent area or an area that's not as comfortable as where you live. Inquiries such as this can keep your sensory exploration muscles working.

Public transportation. Sound and movement. Sound collection is good here. Try a ride home without your ear buds and tune in to the syncopation of bus or train travel. Notice the rebound/space rebound that happens imperceptibly, almost seamlessly. If you always sit, next time choose to stand. Who is too close? How do you decide? Is it when you can smell his aftershave or only when she steps on your toes? Who makes eye contact? How does that feel? Who never looks up? Where do you feel comfort in your body on your commute? Next to a window? Near the conductor or driver?

On a plane. Move like an octopus. If you're lying flat in First Class this is easy, but even in Coach, get up and stretch as you walk to the bathroom, and once inside that bathroom, do a standing octopus shimmy. You'll be lubricating your spine with nourishing cerebrospinal fluid.

Before a Big Meeting, First Impression, or Presentation

Try Bringing Down Heaven, carry a Touchstone, or Stillpoint if you have a few minutes to sit alone beforehand. Focus on finding nature in your immediate environment. Give yourself an Energy Infusion by recalling a major C.

No Trigger—Spouse or Significant Other

Scan your body for the highest concentration of tension. Ask yourself what role your spouse is casting you in or which role you are jumping into before you conclude what action is required. What role can you adopt even briefly to seek common ground? Often the inquiry will help defuse tension. If it's a triangle-based role you feel you need to adopt, just be certain to step away, find Neutral, and reconsider.

No Trigger—Your Boss

First and foremost this is a functional relationship, regardless of any emotional layers that might additionally be present. So practice Neutral. Imagine the space between you and your boss as you would in space rebound. This will slow the whole scene down so you can connect to your breath. Try a belly breath that can be hard if your boss has just said something shocking or inflammatory. Hard, yes, but it's probably exactly what's needed. If your boss makes a demand and waltzes off, this is a perfect opportunity to pull a stone out of your desk and blow your response into that stone, giving that excess steam to the stone. Remember, you move in relationship to the boss's move. That move can be a move away, and just tracking it will allow space for a good response or a neutral move to be made.

No Trigger—The World

This can be complex, but the premise of the 30 days is to create a sacred relationship with your body and see it as a wise ally that has answers if you will only tap in and trust them. Practice envisioning the world as a musically breathing sacred compatriot. How would you feel if that were true? Extend your reach by focusing a fluid awareness on the world. You cannot envision this and stay static or stay triggered by the world.

No Trigger—Everyday Rudeness

Small acts of unkindness, such as someone cutting ahead of you in line, can sometimes set off a disproportionate reaction inside us. Of course, you can choose to track Neutral. However, often, it's the shock value, the unexpected ugliness of a moment that negatively gets to us on a cellular level. If a stranger or a person in a functional role shocks you, immediately place a hand on your throat, heart, or gut, whichever area feels most vulnerable. After a while with working the tools in this book, you'll know specifically where in your body you absorbed the shock of the moment and where your hand needs to go. Then bring a C to mind. If you've previously anchored the C well, your alarm system will lower, your attention will shift, and your mood will lighten or soften. Then, whatever shock your body absorbed from the unpleasant encounter will dissipate.

Family Holiday Dinners

These events are often filled with lots of disparate energy even under the most harmonious of situations. One word: Neutral. Practice finding it. Track it. Live it.

Chronic Illness

Most of what you've learned and folded into your 30 days applies to working with chronic pain. A particularly potent self inquiry is to make a habit of asking each day, "Today, where is health in my body?" Even if it's only your pinky finger that feels good and flexes well, note it. Actively be on the lookout for, and focus gratefully on, the signs of health.

Also, separating out what's yours energetically from what is other can be refreshing. Consider a revamp of your Energy Signature. Ask yourself what would have to change for you to alter your Energy Signature, to help you feel better or like your circumstances more. As always, be sensory and specific.

Self Love

Surround yourself with Touchstones. Identify those relationships that provide true response of the positive/positive variety. Practice Neutral. Make a Transformation Circle. Move like an octopus. Practice Inner Reconnaissance often. Give your uncertainty, your pain, to Mother Earth to mulch for you. Don't concern yourself with how that's going to occur. Do your part by setting Intention, then practice trust. Practice allowing. Look for opportunities to create sacred ceremony, however you'd like that to manifest.

Dealing With Death

Grief is a large subject that cannot be covered within the scope of this book. However, during the stages of grief when we feel "out of our body" and inconsolable or in shock, that's a critical time to do what animals do—husband our resources and conserve our energy. Whether we prefer constant company or removing ourselves from our pack, we need Touchstones and ways to ground so we can avoid accidents and safely release our shock. Introduce a simple ceremony into each day. Repetition can be comforting.

A Word About Ceremony

Any of the tools I've given you can allow the bringing of ceremony into your life on a daily basis. Ceremony can stretch your sense of time, lowering stress. An element of reverence can only enhance your experience of any of the exercises in my system. With that said, I suggest that, rather than viewing any exercise as working for you or not, the ceremonial way to view the entire process would be to enter into the state of awe, to suspend disbelief and work with the tool rather than expecting it to automatically work for you. Guess what happens then? You get deeper, richer results. Your focus is wider, and by adding that element of entering into possibility, which the idea of ceremony encourages, the ordinary becomes extraordinary. This is otherwise known as alchemy.

List of Descriptive, Sensory Words for Use with Exercises

When describing pain, use words to communicate what your body is sharing with you. Instead of simply "It's painful," be descriptive. Remember, your body is listening.

Begin with questioning: Is the pain sharp or dull? Does the sensation move around or stay in one place? Is there a color? Yellow can be golden as well as puke yellow. Red has a different frequency than does crimson, for another example. Be as specific as you can be. Is there a shape? Beyond saying "round," ask your body if there is a fullness or a flatness in your awareness. Is there a sound to the pain? Examples could include:

- shrill
- groaning
- creaky
- humming
- piercing
- monotone

Here is an additional sampling of descriptors for pain or how a body element may feel in a sensory way:

antsy	congealed
aching	crispy
alternating	cold
bubbly	clear
blobby	dull
bitter	dangerous
bumpy	dark
creepy	damp

- ❀ fizzy
- ❀ fake
- ❀ failed
- ❀ frozen
- ❀ forgotten
- ❀ foggy
- ❀ gloomy
- ❀ glittery
- ❀ glistening
- ❀ granulated
- ❀ heavy
- ❀ hollow
- ❀ hand-me-down
- ❀ inky
- ❀ jumpy
- ❀ jittery
- ❀ jarred
- ❀ liquid
- ❀ lumpy
- ❀ lost
- ❀ lingering
- ❀ mangled
- ❀ misty
- ❀ mushy
- ❀ needy
- ❀ original
- ❀ overwhelmed
- ❀ pointed
- ❀ prickly
- ❀ pulsing
- ❀ rough
- ❀ slippery
- ❀ smooth
- ❀ sticky
- ❀ stuck
- ❀ sharp
- ❀ tender
- ❀ uneven
- ❀ undulating
- ❀ urgent
- ❀ wild
- ❀ wispy
- ❀ worried

Here are some additional descriptive words to get you started with making sensory connections:

- ❀ abundant
- ❀ airy
- ❀ angular
- ❀ banded
- ❀ bonded
- ❀ creamy
- ❀ cushy
- ❀ curdled
- ❀ clipped
- ❀ crinkly
- ❀ dazzling
- ❀ dirty
- ❀ eerie
- ❀ energized

- expansive
- fertile
- flowering
- fancy
- fruitful
- flush
- gliding
- golden
- grand
- gritty
- gelatinous
- grizzled
- generous
- hoarse
- joyous
- jello-y
- jumpy
- klutzy
- klunky
- lavish
- lyrical
- loopy
- lemony
- lucky
- leathery
- liquid
- luscious
- languid
- marching
- moon-y
- minty
- mushy
- nicked
- noisy
- open
- original
- overflowing
- peppy
- prickly
- pristine
- quiet
- rich
- ripe
- slinky
- sloshy
- teeming
- thriving
- toxic
- unctuous
- universal
- unlimited
- velvety
- willful
- whimsical
- witty
- zapped
- zingy

Finally, here are some sample phrases to describe how body parts feel (as in a quiz question):

❀ Gliding like a koi fish.

❀ On the prowl like a shark.

❀ Arcing like a dolphin. (All fish are not created equal.)

❀ Buzzing like a bee.

❀ Relentless like a buzz saw. (There is a different quality to the two types of buzzing: nature vs. manmade.)

❀ Swaying like a tree.

❀ Swaying like an elephant's trunk. (See how "swaying" all by itself leaves room for further inquiry?)

❀ Cold, cracked ice.

❀ Smooth, frozen, whipped dessert. (Cold is inherently neither good nor bad.)

Your body lets you know, ultimately, whether you've veered off track or are simply layering a descriptor on. It will take practice before you'll be certain when inquiring on your own body's behalf. In the early explorations, depending on the situation, and certainly in the case of structural problems and complex physical issues, working with a qualified facilitator can be of immense value. See the list of Resources at the end of the book.

As you refer to this book regularly, you have the opportunity to continue getting your habits in sync with your daily life. So much is possible. So much is waiting to be discovered. It's not out there somewhere. Taking responsibility for showing up for yourself can be fun and rewarding, even magical. But as an Inner Alchemist you know that now, don't you.

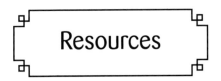

Resources

My Website is *www.cranialalchemy.com*. My mailing address is 13351-D Riverside Drive, # 293, Sherman Oaks, California 91423.

I offer two programs to further support and customize my Alchemy system for you or your group. For information on these modules that enhance this 30-day plan contact: support@thealchemyofself-healing.com.

Receive your free download of the complete Inner Reconnaissance meditation, used throughout your 30-day journey, by visiting my Website and clicking the box marked, "Claim your Meditation Download."

Locate a Craniosacral Therapist in Your Area

Upledger Institute
www.upledger.com
11211 Prosperity Farms Road, Suite D-325
Palm Beach Gardens, Florida 33410
800-233-5880 (toll free)

Silverhorse Healing Ranch
Sara Fancy
The ranch offers a variety of ways to heal with horses.
www.silverhorseranch.org

Biodynamic Resonance Technique

A unique healing approach that utilizes energetically programmed vials to remind the healer within of its innate potential.

West Coast Contact: Dr. Patricia Ebert.

drpattidc@yahoo.com

East Coast Contact: Dr. Dominique Desrochers.

Allhands121@yahoo.com

Inka Medicine Wheel

Delve into your sacred nature.

www.Inkamedicinewheel.com

Tomas Bostrom

Four Winds School

Alberto Viloldo, PhD

www.thefourwinds.com

Renee Le Beau

Acoustic Alchemist

Sound healing with ancient instruments.

www.reneelebeau.com

Sacred Chambers

Oneness University

A divine international phenomenon.

www.onenessuniversity.org

Crystalline Work
Aravel Garduno
Detailed work with codices, crystalline energy.
www.crystallineconsciousnesswork.com

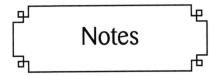

Notes

Chapter 1

1. Viola Spolin, Theatre Games, via George Morrison, Purchase College 1974, *www.spolin.com*.
2. In conversation with the author.
3. Dr. John Upledger's Upledger Institute teaches Dr. Still's Four Tenets in Introductory classes around the world.
4. Yo-Yo Ma, "Behind the Cello," *Huffington Post*, January 21, 2014, *www.huffingtonpost.com*.

Chapter 2

1. David Abram, *The Spell of the Sensuous* (New York: Vintage Books, Random House, 1996), xi, 47.
2. "Sparkle Hip," *Massage Today*, April 2010, *www.massagetoday.com*.
3. Gerald Huther, *The Compassionate Brain*, English translation, (Shambala Publications, 2006), 20.

Chapter 3

1. Joshua Boettiger, "No Ideas But In Things," *Parabola Magazine*, Spring 2013, 30.

2. Genesis 26, Torah, 18–22.

3. Boettiger, "No Ideas But In Things," 31.

4. Abram, *The Spell of the Sensuous*, 33.

Chapter 5

1. Rowan Hooper, "Spectrum of Empathy Found in the Brain," *New Scientist*, September 18, 2006, *www.newscientist.com*.

Chapter 6

1. Marianne Williamson at Vicki Abelson's Women Who Write Salon, April 1, 2014, vickiabelson.com/site/Women_Who_Write/Women_Who_Write.html.

Chapter 7

1. Abram, *The Spell of the Sensuous*, 87.

2. Maurice Merleau-Ponty, *Phenomenology of Perception* (London: Routledge & Keegan Paul, 1962), 233.

3. Bhavika and Clyde, "432Hz Coming Back to Nature," March 13, 2014, *www.fractalenlightenment.com*.

4. "Power of sound for healing our nervous system brain," March 12, 2014, *www.stopthestorm.com*.

5. Itzhak Bentov, *Stalking the Wild Pendulum* (New York: Dutton, 1977), 92.

6. Rhonda Byrne, *The Secret* (Hillsboro, Oregon: Beyond Words Publishing, 2006).

7. Bentov, *Stalking the Wild Pendulum*, 111.

8. Abram, *The Spell of the Sensuous*, 75.

Index

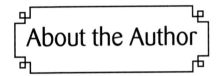

About the Author

As a young girl, Jeannine Wiest wanted to be a detective—first Harriet the Spy and later Emma Peel from the British television show, *The Avengers*.

Born in Lansing, Michigan, Wiest grew up in New York City where she attended the famed High School of the Performing Arts. Rather than becoming a detective, she went on to receive a BFA from Purchase College, which led her to becoming a dancer on Broadway. After moving to Los Angeles, she created a successful design firm, designing one-of-a-kind clothes for boutiques around the world. While working on a British television show, Wiest repurposed materials not meant to be clothing into wearable art. As she went on to work on several other television shows, earning an Emmy nomination, she discovered more and more her ability to make connections between things that were not immediately obvious.

Perhaps, she thought, she was a detective after all.

But throughout these years, Wiest was ill. She was twice diagnosed as having cancer, but she knew the diagnosis wasn't right, and ultimately, after enduring years of pain, she learned she had endometriosis. In seeking alternative treatments, Wiest discovered Craniosacral Therapy. It was only then, as she began listening to her own body, that she healed. Pain-free and impressed by the power of this treatment, she went into training to become a Craniosacral Therapist, Reiki Master, and holistic coach.

One afternoon after dissecting a cadaver in class, Wiest was holding a heart in her hands when she realized this change of direction was not so dramatic a change; human tissue was, she understood, simply another kind of fabric.

Thus the detective and the artist in her joined forces.

For the past decade Wiest has honed her Cranial Alchemy system, showing her clients, in a sensory way, how to repurpose those cellular stories in our bodies that no longer serve us. She has worked with myriad clients, both in groups and one-on-one—everyone from artists, celebrities, and billionaires to corporate escapees to handicapped children in Bali. In every case, she has witnessed the wonder in her clients' eyes as they learn to listen to their bodies, utilizing the tools now available in *The Alchemy of Self Healing*.